The Modern Witch

The Modern Witch

Understanding Contemporary Witchcraft and Wicca

THORN MOONEY

JAICO PUBLISHING HOUSE

Ahmedabad Bangalore Chennai
Delhi Hyderabad Kolkata Mumbai

Published by Jaico Publishing House
A-2 Jash Chambers, 7-A Sir Phirozshah Mehta Road
Fort, Mumbai - 400 001
jaicopub@jaicobooks.com
www.jaicobooks.com

Published in arrangement with
Llewellyn Publications
2143 Wooddale Drive, Woodbury
Minnesota 55125-2989, USA
www.llewellyn.com

To be sold only in India, Pakistan, Nepal,
Burma, Bangladesh, Thailand, and Sri Lanka.

THE MODERN WITCH
ISBN 978-93-49358-85-0

Original English language edition published as
Witches Among Us

First Jaico Impression: 2025

Printed by
Trinity Academy For Corporate Training Limited, Mumbai

Dedication

For Elisabeth, Gina, and Bee

Acknowledgments

This has been a very different sort of book from my earlier works, and it's been both gratifying and enormously challenging both to write for a wider audience and to try and represent an entire movement, rather than only my own little corner of it. It's always tricky walking the line between insider and outsider, and I'm only able to do so thanks to a number of friends and mentors.

To my friends, colleagues, and peers at Llewellyn, especially Elysia, Lauryn, Markus, and Leah, for everything from patience and expertise to encouragement, laughs, memes, inspiration, books, and snacks. The roster of Llewellyn authors I have the privilege of hanging out with and learning from continues to be bewildering, and I'm so grateful to share shelves with you all.

To the witches from other traditions who provided their expertise, read drafts, suggested resources, and provided nuance, especially Jack, Tom, Gwion, and Kelden.

To my academic mentors and friends, who encouraged me, gave me the space to work on this project, and were enthusiastic when I was not, especially Randall (who has the distinction of being the voice I hear in my head). Big shout-out to Mackenzie and Jacob, who are the very best thing about doctor school.

To the witches of Foxfire, Corvinian, Hawkfire, and Kithic. Everything is for you, always.

To Corvus, who is always the first person I share my work with, and from whom I've probably learned more about life and magic than anyone.

To my mom and dad, who are patient and kind and have always supported me.

And to Matt, of course. Finest of humans, best of partners, favorite of cats (and me).

Contents

Introduction

October hits and, as surely as the calendar scrolls forward, the tone of my inbox shifts. Interspersed with messages from students asking about midterms and invitations to Halloween parties are requests from journalists, podcasters, and internet personalities looking for someone to talk to about witchcraft. The questions they ask are different depending on their angle. Those who find me through my university credentials ask me to explain why witches seem to be everywhere these days or why anyone reasonable might want to become a witch. Those who find me through my platform on social media, where I'm openly a Wiccan high priestess, want to know what witches are *really* up to. And—without fail—whether or not spells actually work! These latter requests sometimes border on sensationalism, but more often than not, they take the position of declaring that witches, whatever the media might lead us to believe, are no different from the rest of us. Neither angle is entirely true. Or, perhaps, both are equally true. The residual fear and curiosity surrounding witchcraft still makes for good clickbait each year, but it's also strangely ubiquitous these days, and often framed as a quirky distraction for rebellious teen girls or an eccentric pursuit popular with granola moms and hippie types. Stereotypes abound, and most of them are some flavor of disparaging. The real picture is quite a bit more complicated.

In most ways I look very conventional from the outside. I was raised by a nice family in an American suburb, graduated from a state university, and entered the workforce. I've variously been a classroom teacher, a retail worker, a corporate office employee, and a graduate student. Most of the people I've met in these realms would not suspect that I have another life entirely. I began exploring the world of magic, witchcraft, and the occult as a youngster, driven—like many children—by an interest in mythology, fantasy, and storytelling. As a teenage girl, I was introduced more seriously to witchcraft through a combination of television and movies (the nineties were something of a hotbed for witch depictions) and the influence of equally fascinated friends. The witchcraft books we were reading promised that witchcraft could improve our personal lives, help us connect to the cycles of nature, and tap into extraordinary magical abilities. By the time I entered college, I identified as a witch and had aspirations to take on leadership positions in the magical communities I was frequenting. I participated in a campus Pagan student club, attended open rituals at a local metaphysical store, and spent the summers traveling to magical festivals. I would in short order become an initiate in a coven, then many years later a high priestess, and finally a coven leader in my own right. I practiced spells, led nighttime rituals, spoke to spirits and gods, and performed secret rites passed to me by a line of magical elders.

I wrote books and articles showing others how to do the same and began speaking and teaching at many of the events I had attended as a young person.

The entire time, every weekday morning, I donned business casual, made coffee, and went to work a totally conventional job, just like millions of other people. In this way I was (and still am) both extraordinary and completely unremarkable. As a scholar, I have an academic history that may be a little unconventional—I specialize in religion and culture, which includes everything from evangelical megachurches to paranormal television shows—but you'd have a hard time picking me out of a crowd. Yet witchcraft is one of the most significant parts of my life, impacting everything from my personal relationships to my career choices. Most of the people I encounter in my day-to-day have no idea that they know a witch.

It's very likely that you know a witch too. It's very likely, in fact, that you know more than one—if not immediately in your most intimate spaces, at least in passing. Perhaps at work or at school, while socializing among casual acquaintances, or while enjoying your favorite media. If nowhere else, witches are seemingly everywhere in television, movies, and music. If you're active in digital spaces, you may have noticed an increase in mentions related to witches and witchcraft on your social media feeds. It's not uncommon to see speculations surrounding the supposed magical inclination of popular celebrities right alongside self-identified witches proudly claiming to have hexed offending politicians. You may also have heard the term "Wicca," if not from a practitioner directly, then perhaps from one of those October newspaper features I mentioned, a comparative religions textbook in college, or one of myriad online stories about the freedom of religious expression in classrooms, prisons, or courtrooms. You may have heard that Wicca is a kind of witchcraft or even that these terms are interchangeable (they aren't, but we'll get to that later).

Aside from knowing a witch or two, it's equally likely that those in your life don't fit neatly into any given stereotype, of which there are several. While it's true that academic studies of practitioners of witchcraft have observed certain patterns in demographics, the myriad types of witchcraft that have blossomed in recent decades ensure that there is no singular image we could point to with any certainty. Witches don't necessarily look a particular way or come from a particular background. They might occupy any number of professions, have diverse educational histories, and seem to be just as likely to live in small towns as big cities. Some practitioners are vocal and visible, but many more are intensely private and prefer not to share their beliefs and practices with others. Some are members of groups and larger organizations made up of other witches, but many are solitary, making it nearly impossible to estimate a population size with any accuracy. We can make reasonable guesses based on metaphysical book sales, online polling, and attendance at witch-related events, but the decentralized nature of witchcraft and the fuzziness surrounding what constitutes membership and practice versus curiosity and experimentation means that we're sure to be wrong, and perhaps significantly so.

Witches and witchcraft are increasingly visible in social, political, and commercial spaces. The language of witchcraft has seeped into public life, and many of its beliefs and practices have entered the mainstream. Popular magazines, television shows, and literature routinely include discussions of real witchcraft, as well as witch characters modeled after contemporary witches. Celebrities promote healing techniques long connected to magic and the occult, and corporate culture includes manifestation and meditation among more routine productivity strategies. Even people who don't think of themselves as religious or magical sometimes turn to astrology or tarot cards for guidance in their daily lives. None of these things individually is witchcraft, but together they indicate a shifting cultural climate in which magical thinking thrives. The presence of magical and esoteric themes in everyday life spurs the rising popularity of witchcraft as a subject and increases interest among would-be practitioners. It also points to a rapidly growing consumer market. What has come to be called the "witch aesthetic"—think flowy black fabrics, mushroom and greenery prints, and oddities like animal skulls and crystals—has crept into fashion, interior decorating, and all kinds of visual art. Popular brands attempt to cater to consumers interested in magic at every turn, and witchcraft books and tools feature on endcaps at major retailers.

It seems probable that witchcraft communities will continue to grow and develop, and that witchcraft will continue to expand into mainstream spaces. The rising popularity of witchcraft and related traditions potentially impacts all kinds of social arenas, from workplaces and classrooms to consumer markets and popular media. A working familiarity with this body of traditions and the people who practice them (or are simply fascinated by them) is increasingly important, especially when so much misinformation circulates. And if you've got a witch or two in your personal life, learning something about this rapidly growing movement is even more pressing.

This book is designed to help you navigate this complex world, whether someone in your life has just revealed that they are a witch, you deal with witches and witchcraft in some professional or community capacity, or you're just witch-curious. Even though it might seem like witches and witchcraft have become mainstream, it can be extremely overwhelming orienting yourself. Social media is full of conflicting information, and the thousands of books on the market today are almost entirely written for people who are either already practitioners or who aspire to be. This book is for everyone else.

In the following chapters, we'll briefly look at the many meanings of the word "witch," some of the histories of contemporary witchcraft, the kinds of witchcraft that people practice today, what doing witchcraft includes, and how witch communities are structured. We'll take a look at the most common objects used in witchcraft, familiarize ourselves with various kinds of witchcraft rituals, and take a close look at how witches use magic and what magic actually entails. Finally, we'll examine some of the social issues currently surrounding witchcraft communities. Because the world of witchcraft is as diverse and changeable as the people who inhabit it, no single book could ever fairly represent absolutely everyone. Even the most definitive descriptions I provide for you here are sure to have exceptions in the lived experiences of individual witches, and for that reason you'll also leave with resources for where to go next if you decide you would like to keep learning. Every chapter ends with both primary and secondary resources for your consideration so you can choose from a selection of related scholarly materials or read the words of witches themselves (and I encourage you to do both). These latter works offer perspectives that may conflict with one another and represent different regions, time periods, and cultural contexts. This display of variety is intentional. As you read this book, you may at times find yourself wishing for fast and concise answers and more clearly constructed definitions and boundaries, but to force witches and their myriad traditions, ideas, and communities into such a neat package would be deceptive and ultimately unhelpful. What I offer you here is a map—not the territory itself.

As your guide, I'll be wearing two hats and walking the line between two perspectives. First, as a religious studies scholar, I am able to construct a bigger picture, framing witchcraft within a wider spiritual and cultural landscape. Witchcraft means many things to many different people, and witchcraft today has a number of connections within other esoteric, magical, and religious movements. Where the lines are between witchcraft and these other movements is always up for debate, especially among practitioners. Not all witches agree on matters of history, theology, ritual practice, identity, and community. My scholarly training allows me to navigate many of these differences, drawing distinctions and connections that will help you be able to spot contradictions when you encounter them and avoid unnecessary confusion. Second, as a longtime practitioner with experience in multiple traditions, I am able to offer a level of nuance that is unavailable to most outsiders writing about witchcraft. These communities are important to me on a deeply personal level, and how they are represented in media affects me directly, at every level of my life. These perspectives combine to allow for a rare glimpse into the intricacies of this rich, challenging, and surprisingly prescient world that holds such intense appeal for so many.

Chapter 1

What "Witch" Means

When I call myself a witch, I mean a lot of different things all at once. I have used the word countless times in response to questions like, "Are you religious?" and "Do you think of yourself as spiritual?" (as well as the all too common, "What church do you belong to?"). I answer a little differently depending on whom I'm talking to and what assumptions and experiences I think they're working with. Most of the time on standardized questionnaires that ask about religious affiliation—like those you might see on government forms, census polling, or university demographics studies—I'm forced to check a box simply labeled "other." On rare occasions—though they are becoming more frequent, as times change—I am offered the option of "New Age" or "Neo-Pagan." I may or may not check either of these descriptors, depending on how expansive I'm feeling that day. Neither feels perfectly accurate in my case, though other witches may embrace one or both of these terms enthusiastically. Others openly resent being lumped in, feeling that witchcraft is something else entirely (some of those witches probably refused to even fill out the survey, on principle).

If I'm among more familiar company, I'll explain that I'm a witch, and more specifically that I'm a practitioner of a particular type of witchcraft called Wicca. Wicca is one of the most visible types of contemporary witchcraft and has a history of appearing in the public eye as a religion, if perhaps an unusual one. Usually, my conversation partners have heard of it, even if they may not be entirely clear on what it entails. If I find myself in the company of someone who has a bit more knowledge—maybe a fellow religious studies scholar or a fellow magical practitioner—I'll be even more specific and say that I'm a Gardnerian Wiccan. Like most any other religion we could name, Wicca comes in flavors, and I belong to one specifically. You are likely familiar with the role of denominations in Christianity, and Wicca is much the same, except we mostly use the word "tradition" to describe our different types.

But "witch" is much bigger than "Wicca"—many if not most witches today are not Wiccan—and when I call myself a witch, I mean so much more (and I was a witch long before I became a Gardnerian Wiccan). I use the word to also mean that I'm an occultist (not all occultists are witches, but in my own life these things are closely linked). Occultism is about what is hidden, and witchcraft is one of the hidden arts.[1] I believe that the world is bigger and more complicated than we can always articulate and that there are unseen forces at work that make the seemingly impossible possible. I also—and perhaps most importantly—

1. We'll talk more about both Wicca and occultism in the coming sections and in the next chapter.

use the word to mean that I practice magic. Witchcraft is a skill set that allows me to interact with those unseen forces, and it's something that I actively work at—learning as much as I can, experimenting, swapping experiences with other witches, and *practicing*. We cast spells; conduct rituals; practice herbal medicine; communicate with ancestors, gods, and other kinds of spirits; and study the past to connect with histories and traditions that have been oppressed, erased, or neglected at the feet of a seemingly disenchanted modernity. Finally, when I call myself a witch, I'm consciously setting myself apart from the status quo. I feel innately different from other kinds of people, and witchcraft gives me the language to articulate that difference. The witch is an outsider figure and has served as a symbol for marginalized groups of many kinds. The witch has been a rallying figure for feminists, for queer communities, and for individuals who exist on the fringes, unable or unwilling to conform to societal expectations. When I call myself a witch, I am indicating my magical inclinations, my religious persuasion, and also my pride in my individuality and sense of belonging to outsider communities. When someone calls themselves a witch, they could mean any or all of these.

Is witchcraft a religion? Yes, except for when it's definitely not. Is it an inherent identity—something you're born with, or something you discover? Maybe, but if it is, it's also something someone can cultivate and claim, regardless of their background (though it's surely fair to say that some will come to it more easily than others). Is it just a mechanical practice or a tool kit, like being able to fix home appliances or learning how to bake? For some witches, yes, but even when we call witchcraft a "practice" or a "craft," it still carries the cultural weight of something deeply meaningful, carefully learned, and artfully administered. Witchcraft is defined differently by individuals operating in different spaces, and contemporary witch communities present us with contradictions and disagreements, all while they share so much and are recognizably related. In this chapter, we'll take a close look at the many ways that witches characterize their craft: as religion, as spirituality, as practice, and as identity. Not merely a question of semantics, these deceptively small differences represent a matter of intense debate among practitioners and are the source of much confusion for anyone trying to learn about witchcraft today. We'll approach all these terms as fluid and imperfect. Witches tend to choose their words with care, and their choices about these nebulous categories can tell us quite a lot about their individual experiences, beliefs, and values.

Before we begin, for the purposes of our explorations in this short book, one parameter will remain consistent: the identity of "witch" is one that must be self-owned and self-applied. Witchcraft is everything I have described thus far, but it's also historically an accusation and a condemnation. Even today, in some parts of the world witch hunting is a very real phenomenon that carries potentially deadly consequences. "Witch" is an insult hurled by outsiders, confronted by something they do not respect or understand. Colonizers encountering religious and cultural others have used "witchcraft" to characterize peoples and practices they deem inferior or "primitive," and even the well-meaning today sometimes conflate the world's many magical traditions, ignoring the boundaries that especially marginalized communities set for themselves. This isn't something I seek to repeat. Limiting the scope of this book to today's self-described witches also means that this isn't a history of witch hunting or witch trials, nor is it a commentary on the continued violent persecution of accused witches in India, Papua New Guinea, Ghana, and elsewhere. The relationship between historical understandings of witchcraft around the world and the contemporary usage of the term by people today is not necessarily continuous. Many good resources exist for readers interested in these other cases, but my focus is on the witches and witchcraft that you are most likely to encounter today.

Making Witchcraft a Religion

Contemporary witches of many varieties consider witchcraft to be their religion. Though in recent years, a rapidly growing number of practitioners eschew the category (for reasons we'll get into shortly), the notion that witchcraft is a religious movement has dominated much of the popular conversation for decades. Many of the most popular books produced by witches in the last seventy or so years have described witchcraft as a religion, not unlike other religions with which you may already be familiar. Indeed, many witchcraft traditions include the typical markers that we look for when we collectively describe religion: rules and organizational structures, beliefs about gods and afterlives, a shared ethical code, rituals pertaining to life events like marriages and births, and a set of sacred holidays equipped with their own liturgies and celebratory rites. If you were to take a class on new religious movements offered at a university or read a book about "world religions," you would likely encounter Wicca or contemporary Paganism, two related movements that have defined much of what many religion experts think of when they think of "modern witchcraft." You may have seen news stories about witches asserting their right to the same freedoms and protections offered to other religious groups, especially in the United States. This is significant because the conversation surrounding whether or not witchcraft is a religion isn't just a matter of the presence of deities, ethical codes, or organizational structures; calling something a religion (or deciding that something *isn't* religion) is also fundamentally a political decision, and one with potentially significant social consequences.[2]

The first books advocating for and describing the practice of contemporary witchcraft, published by the British witch Gerald Gardner and his contemporaries, were published after the repeal of the United Kingdom's Witchcraft Act of 1735 in 1951. It might be difficult for many of us today to conceive of witchcraft as a crime punishable under the law, but this was the reality for practitioners even into the twentieth century, and this was the backdrop of the witchcraft movement as it developed in Britain. For Gardner and many of the other witches writing, speaking, and spreading contemporary witchcraft, their traditions were not merely the practice of magic but actually the survival of a pre-Christian religion with roots in the Neolithic. The idea that witchcraft is a religion in and of itself—rather than a Christian heresy, a reinterpreted folk practice, a deviant magical system, or a superstitious misunderstanding of natural phenomena—takes root in the twentieth century, thanks in large part to the work of scholar Margaret Murray. Murray is famous today for

2. A number of well-circulated scholars have written about religion and its connection to power, authority, and the state, including Naomi Goldenberg, Malory Nye, and Jason Bivins. For a broad and engaging conversation about the boundaries around how we define religion, consider *What Is Religion?: Debating the Academic Study of Religion*, edited by Aaron Hughes and Russell McCutcheon (Oxford: Oxford University Press, 2021).

what is sometimes called "the Murray thesis" or "the witch-cult hypothesis," which she articulated in her books *The Witch-Cult in Western Europe* (1921) and *The God of the Witches* (1931).[3] Murray described a witch religion that venerated a god of hunting, animals, and wild spaces and a goddess of the moon, magic, and fertility. This became the foundation for Gardner and for many other witches operating during this period, inspiring not only what would come to be called Wicca (a tradition explicitly rooted in Gardner's work) but also other traditions of witchcraft. Understanding witchcraft as a religion was, for many of these early witches, a way to reclaim a lost history (however romanticized), to reclaim a sense of connection to the land they lived on, and also to rail against the disenchantment brought about by both industrialization and disillusionment with the religious paradigms that had dominated up to that point.

The move to have witchcraft defined as religion has been a lengthy, complicated battle born out of a need to provide legal protection for practitioners in public spaces, like schools, the military, and the workplace. One noteworthy case occurred in 2007 when the United States Department of Veterans Affairs made the pentacle—the five-pointed star enclosed in a circle widely used by many kinds of witches—available for use on headstones at Arlington National Cemetery. Service members can designate "Wiccan" and "Pagan" on their dog tags, kids at American public schools can't be bullied or suspended for wearing pentacle jewelry, and workers can take their holidays off the

3. The witch-cult hypothesis did not originate with Murray, but the popularity of her work and its impact on contemporary witches has cemented her position and ensured that her name is the first invoked in any discussion of witchcraft as a pre-Christian religious survival.

same way other religious groups take time off for their own seasonal celebrations. All of these are comparatively recent developments, largely born out of lawsuits filed in response to workplace and school persecutions against individual practitioners.

These efforts became especially important in the wake of what has come to be called the Satanic Panic, a moral panic that arose in the 1980s in the United States but quickly spread internationally. Allegations of Satanic ritual abuse against children featured in mainstream television and publishing, triggered by the publication of *Michelle Remembers* by Michelle Smith and Lawrence Pazder. Conspiracy theories abounded, and investigations pertaining to supposed Satanic ritual abuse impacted schools and families in the United States and beyond. At the same time, Fundamentalist minister and popular televangelist Jerry Falwell's Moral Majority was bringing a particular kind of politically engaged, conservative Christianity to the fore of American media in unprecedented ways. Suspicions rose surrounding anything deemed Satanic, which, according to popular materials circulating at the time, might include fantasy role-playing games, an interest in the occult, Goth and punk subcultures, heavy metal music, and much more. As bewildering as some of this may sound today, these impulses held real consequences for the accused, and the repercussions of this period are still impacting people today. Contemporary witches, Pagans, and occultists faced real threats to their jobs, their families, and their physical safety. These anxieties were amplified again with the 1999 shooting at Columbine High School in Colorado, which further fanned moral panic in the United States around both Goth and heavy metal subcultures and occult symbolism. If witchcraft collectively could be framed as religion in a legal sense, this ostensibly offered more protection for practitioners who feared becoming the targets of this sort of fearmongering.

One of the difficulties and discomforts surrounding witchcraft as a "religion" lies in cultural biases pertaining to the definition of religion as a category. Most of our popular definitions of religion are rooted in normative social and legal parameters that take Christianity, and especially Protestant Christianity, as the definitive model. Whether or not we come to understand something as religion has historically been a matter of determining how closely something resembles the Christianity that has defined the Western world.[4] Witchcraft—even that witchcraft practiced under the auspices of religion by witches who call themselves religious—doesn't necessarily behave the way outsiders might expect, given how we tend to use monotheistic traditions as our sole models. Witches tend to emphasize ritual practice over maintaining specific beliefs, for example (you are much more likely to hear witches ask each other about what they *do* rather than what they *believe*). They also are likely to practice alone, without ever joining established groups akin to churches or temples.

Most witches who believe in deities or spirits also believe that they can interact with them directly, unmediated, and thus there is not necessarily a need for what we would conventionally think of as clergy. Their moral codes are often private and self-determined, rather than prescribed by established authorities or shared sacred texts. In fact, most witches don't work from shared sacred texts (though they may write their own)! In

4. For more on this as well as the role that colonialism has played in the development of world religions as a concept, consider Tomoko Masuzawa's *The Invention of World Religions* (Chicago: University of Chicago Press, 2005).

the growing number of cases where witches have organized to behave more like Christian traditions—forming churches and seminaries and adopting titles like "minister" or training to fulfill the role of chaplains or counselors—they have often done so for the sake of legal recognition, protection, and advocacy in the face of systems that tend to assume these models are normative. Thus, even where witchcraft is a religion, it does not necessarily resemble what might initially come to mind! Nonetheless, for those witches who identify as religious, their traditions are as rich, deep, and fulfilling as those of any other religious movement.

Spiritual but Not Religious

Practically any popular news source you'd care to peruse has run stories in recent years about the decline of religion among the citizens of various wealthy nations, especially the United States and the United Kingdom. Attendance at many kinds of religious services has declined, and young people in particular are less likely to identify as members of specific traditions, describing themselves as unaffiliated or indicating that religion just isn't very important to them. Scholars, journalists, and popular opinion point to a number of factors to explain this: scientific advancement and improvement in education, increased globalization and exposure to new ideas, the failure of older religious groups to recruit new members, the COVID-19 pandemic decreasing willingness to go to conventional services in person, and the rise of intense individualism that makes us less likely to want to join groups or sacrifice our personal interests. Some of these explanations are more persuasive than others, but the pattern remains. Collectively, a rising number of us seem to be less religious than in previous generations. But does that mean that nothing has taken its place? Are we just not doing *anything*?

Well, no. In fact, in some ways, we're actually doing a lot *more*. Collectively, we're reframing our practices, engaging in more combinative traditions, participating in less hierarchical organizations (and maybe not in organizations at all), and using sometimes very different vocabulary—the language of *spirituality*. More and more, we're identifying as spiritual but not religious. This is especially true for many people who identify as witches. Many witches actively eschew the word "religion" to describe their practices and traditions. They do this for a number of reasons. Many practitioners come to witchcraft because they have left the religions of their birth. Most of us are not born among witch families (though more and more are with each generation!), and many who discover witchcraft in their adulthood come with religious wounds and traumas. Seeking not to replicate the organizational structures, restrictions, hierarchies, or theologies of their previous groups, they are drawn to the independence, creativity, and freedom that witchcraft can offer. Religion might be something permanently tied to rules, and because witchcraft is typically very different, the category just doesn't fit. This sentiment is shared by many spiritual seekers, whether or not they are converts or have experiences in organized religious traditions.

Increasingly, many people are exploring traditions and practices that fulfill many of the same needs that we associate with religion—like a sense of community, a feeling of connection or purpose, and personal well-being. Many types of witchcraft variously emphasize self-awareness, healing, physical wellness, a connection to nature, and personal empowerment, all without the boundaries that we tend to associate with religion. For many witches, spirituality is personal in a way that religion isn't. Spirituality creates a stronger sense of freedom and allows for the celebration of individuality, changing and growing along with each person who engages it. For these practitioners, it is authentic in a way that religion may not be.

Witches who describe their craft as spiritual are likely to enjoy exploring a variety of practices and traditions, both within witchcraft and from complementary systems. Spirituality is often framed as a process of *seeking*. As one grows, learns more, and develops into a more self-actualized person, spirituality often posits that one's practices will shift and change in kind. These practitioners may draw from a variety of religious traditions, they may adopt assorted healing modalities in a quest for personal well-being, and they are likely to prefer unmediated personal experiences, rather than those facilitated by hierarchies, prescribed texts, or strict organizations. Witchcraft as spirituality is deeply personal, fluid, and eclectic, as flexible and creative as the individual witch.

Witchcraft as a Practice

For a growing number of practitioners, witchcraft is a secular practice, devoid of religious elements unless the individual witch opts to incorporate them. As implied in the name, witchcraft is a *craft* and not religion or spirituality. It is a skillset, an art, and a framework that allows practitioners to improve their lives and change the world around them through magic. To be a witch is to practice practical magic—spells and rites that center the pragmatic day-to-day of life, like work, finances, love, family, health, justice, protection, luck, and more. Individual witches may pull from cultural systems they belong to (which might include religion), or learn herbalism, energy healing, divination, or an infinite number of other practical techniques in order to improve their lives and their communities. The do-it-yourself ethic that characterizes witchcraft means that every practitioner is in charge of defining their own parameters. Thus, witchcraft is not inherently any singular thing, religious, spiritual, or otherwise. Some witches explicitly call themselves secular witches, while others might call themselves "non-religious."[5]

The perspective that witchcraft is a neutral practice and not a religion allows for a great deal of flexibility and versatility. Witches may come from any sociocultural location and their practice can reflect their own histories, needs, and values without the imposition of boundaries that the category of religion often implies. Secular and non-religious witches are not beholden to any particular paradigm, so their individual practices may change and conform to the uniqueness of the individual witch. As we touched on in a previous section, the intersection of religion with state regulation is such that choosing to remain outside of it is often by itself a political statement, even sometimes

5. These terms may or may not be interchangeable, depending on who is using them. Sometimes "secular" carries an additional layer of conscious choice and even political weight, especially in the United States, which historically has struggled to consistently define the role of religion in public spaces. Similarly, individual witches may identify as atheists, but this is also not consistently used as a synonym for "secular." Because religious witches tend to prioritize practice over belief, a witch who does not believe in or worship deities may still identify as religious. Paradoxically, in witchcraft spaces, the term "atheist" is sometimes in and of itself a kind of religious identity (specifically one without gods), rather than a term indicating the absence of religion (which includes ritual practice, community belonging, and other elements beyond a belief in deities).

an inadvertent one. Many vocal proponents of secular witchcraft belong to marginalized communities that have previously suffered subjugation at the hands of oppressive governmental policies, colonial states, and other forms of institutionalized control.

If religion is at least in part about sorting people into manageable categories and determining who deserves state protection and who does not, then the choice to defy the category, adopt different language, and reject conventional definitions of religion potentially becomes an act of sovereignty. Witchcraft—both historically and as defined by most contemporary witches—exists on the margins, in wild spaces, among variously marginalized peoples, outside of the regulating light of the village. For some witches, declaring their practice secular is merely a pragmatic and straightforward reflection of their own understanding of what constitutes religion: if religion is about deities and rules and afterlives and anointed leaders, then when those things are absent, they are not doing religion. For others, the declaration is one of conscious defiance, especially as some of the more prominent flavors of witchcraft (like some kinds of Wicca) have entered mainstream consumer spaces and no longer possess the marginalized, secretive ethos that previously attracted so many to their practice.

Even where witches do not use the language of secularism, and even where they do specifically identify as religious or spiritual, the emphasis on practice—*doing*—is almost universal. Witchcraft is an action, and it's one that we get better at over time, with repetition. Social media abounds with information produced by witch content creators, teaching newcomers how to work spells, how to discover and harness the magical properties of plants and stones, how to interpret signs and symbols, what actions to take to make contact with particular deities and spirits (if deities and spirits are involved—for secular witches, this is not the case), and how to develop the discernment to determine where and how they may have gone wrong when their workings fail. A perusal of witchcraft spaces and witchcraft texts is likely to turn up phrases like, "Practicing witchcraft is work," or "If you want to grow as a witch, you need to practice!" When witches meet each other, they will often ask, "How long have you been practicing?" or "What sort of witchcraft do you do?" All of these imply action! Most witches, regardless of how else they identify, use the language of practice, craft, and art to describe their traditions.

The shift in the language surrounding the religiosity or secular nature of witchcraft represents a noteworthy change in recent years, and one that sometimes throws scholars, journalists, and other sorts of outsiders for a loop. Since the so-called "witchcraft revival" of the mid-twentieth century and the prevalence of the witchcraft traditions codified by prominent early witch authors, most of whom described witchcraft as a pre-Christian religious survival, the religiousness of witchcraft has been somewhat taken for granted. This has been especially exacerbated by the prominence of Wicca in the public eye. Wicca, the name of the tradition that developed from the work of Gerald Gardner and many of his contemporaries writing during this period, is a self-consciously religious tradition of witchcraft, and historically many practitioners (and the people writing about them) have used these terms interchangeably. We'll touch on some of the specifics of Wicca's development and influence in subsequent chapters, but for now the important thing to understand is that it only represents one sort of witchcraft. In the same way that football is a sport, but not all sports are football, Wicca is a form of witchcraft that dominated public magical spaces for decades. Though other forms of witchcraft have always existed, these have rarely enjoyed (or, perhaps, suffered) the extensive media attention that Wicca has commanded. Thus, the openly religious nature of Wicca has inadvertently been transposed onto other traditions and practitioners that practice and identify differently.

Witches who declare that witchcraft is secular are as vocal and insistent as those who claim it is religion or spirituality, and a cursory exploration of social media and recent books seems to indicate that their numbers are growing. This shift is as much about generational change as it is a shift in how witches actually practice—what they're doing, what texts they're consuming, and what they value. Previous generations of witches and Pagans were deeply invested in state recognition as a means of protection during a tumultuous period that left many both feeling unsafe and under genuine threat of persecution. Younger generations of witches live in a different world. Witchcraft social media reaches audiences of millions, witchcraft supplies represent a massive consumer market, and witchcraft-related books regularly chart bestseller lists in multiple genres. While persecution still happens—especially among witches who belong to other marginalized communities—witches today enjoy a kind of safety in many public spaces that they did not in the previous century. This naturally leads to new ways of defining and presenting witchcraft, both within witch communities and to outsiders.

Witchcraft as an Identity

Witches frame their craft as religion, as spirituality, and as practice—sometimes all at the same time, and sometimes adamantly one and not the others—but underlying each of these is the sense that witchcraft is for people who are *different*. In many religious traditions, members speak of conversion, or else partake in various kinds of rituals that clearly mark belonging. In witchcraft, however, practitioners are more likely to speak in terms of having always had an awareness that they didn't quite fit in. Many witches point to a sense of otherness that began in childhood or a series of experiences that perhaps led them to believe that they had abilities or an innate relationship with the world (especially the natural world) that the people around them did not. A great number of introductory witchcraft books begin with the author relating tales of childhood bullying for perceived weirdness, near-death experiences, encounters with a ghost or spirit, or the seeming power to work magic without even consciously trying to do so. Our individual stories of finding witchcraft (if we were not born to witch families) often include narratives that span lengthy periods of time in which we were gradually led to the conclusion that witchcraft was somehow in us all along. If you were to ask, many practitioners will tell you that witchcraft felt like coming home, and that the process of identifying as a witch was one of recognition and familiarity, rather than a conversion or a singular decision. One need not adopt a drastically different lifestyle or make dramatic changes to one's values and beliefs, according to many practitioners—instead, witchcraft just *fits*.

These sorts of narratives, which are typical in witchcraft communities, reflect a collective understanding of witchcraft as fundamentally an identity, rather than either a religion or a practice as we typically understand those terms. In some witchcraft traditions, especially those that are passed along familial lines or cultural lines, this manifests through an emphasis on blood, shared cultural experience, generational trauma, or other matters of ancestry. Witchcraft is inherited, recognized, claimed or reclaimed, and permanently a part of the practitioner regardless of what other routes their life might take, or whether or not they choose to embrace their magical inheritance. In other traditions—for example, those heavily influenced by the feminist movement—practitioners believe that witchcraft is inherently tied to womanhood. These assertions have also made their way into the marketplace, where they have influenced a growing number of people to identify as witches as a matter of social defiance. You may have seen graphic t-shirts and bumper stickers with phrases like, "There's a little witch in every woman," or "We are the granddaughters of the witches you couldn't burn." Here, the witch is innately tied to gender-based oppression and becomes a rallying cry for all women, regardless of whether or not they individually practice magic, adhere to particular witchcraft traditions, or maintain beliefs we typically see among practicing witches. These witches—who may not use the language of practice at all—root their witchcraft in an ideological stance tied innately to gender and to their own conceptions of womanhood under patriarchy.

Other witches center other identities in their description of the boundaries surrounding witchcraft. Some communities and individuals center queer identities and experiences or neurodivergent identities and experiences. For others, the practice of witchcraft necessarily belongs to people of color, historically stripped of agency by colonialism and white supremacy. The fact that witchcraft historically has been tied to the marginalized means that the identity of the witch is often openly linked to those communities and peoples who are oppressed, dismissed, objectified, or denied by those in power and the status quo. This means that the witch potentially becomes a symbol of power for a number of sometimes very different communities, even among those in conflict with each other.[6] Mostly, however, the variety of identities associated with witchcraft (and assumed to be inherent, according to some practitioners) has also encouraged community-wide conversations surrounding intersectionality and social justice, as we recognize our differences and seek to share space with one another under the banner of witchcraft.

Many books about witchcraft begin with a neat definition, and perhaps that is what you had hoped for! Believe me, sometimes I wish it were that simple. Both my personal and my professional lives would be much easier if I could concisely summarize the contemporary witchcraft movement in a handful of sentences and accompanied by a clear diagram, checking a comforting box and drawing familiar comparisons. But the truth is that any attempt to codify witchcraft into a neat, organized category is destined to fail, and even making the attempt does an enormous disservice to the rich, deep, diverse, and ever-expanding realm that witches occupy. Individual witches reach their own conclusions, craft their own definitions, and maintain those boundaries based on experiences and beliefs that are never universal. Contemporary witchcraft includes many people from many sociocultural locations, with different histories, different concerns,

6. One example of this is visible in the use of the witch among trans-exclusive feminist groups and individuals, who see themselves as somehow being marginalized by queer and trans practitioners. Suffice it to say that identifying as a witch does not ensure the absence of bigotry.

and different strategies for navigating the world. We can observe patterns and make reasonable statements about tendencies, but sometimes that is *all* we can do. We could point to some voices over others and collect evidence to make a strong case for any of the above perspectives—religion, spirituality, practice, identity—to the exclusion of the others, but only if we willfully ignore whole groups of practitioners, and sometimes even entire traditions of witchcraft. It is infinitely more productive to think of witchcraft as rhizomatic: dispersed among many communities, touching many disparate realms of people's lives, overlapping, conflicting, changing, and operating both above ground where we can clearly see it and obscured down in the dirt. In the next chapter, we'll consider witchcraft in context, taking a look at some of its histories, its language, and the neighboring movements that helped to shape it.

Suggested Reading

From Scholars

Please note that most of the scholarly work currently available pertaining to contemporary witchcraft operates from the perspective that witchcraft is a Pagan (sometimes called Neo-Pagan) religion. As we've seen, this is not necessarily reflective of how all witches themselves describe and understand their traditions today.

Drawing Down the Moon: Witches, Druids, Goddess-Worshippers and Other Pagans in America, revised and updated edition, by Margot Adler (New York: Penguin, 2006)

Adler was an esteemed news correspondent for NPR, and this text, originally published in 1979, remains one of the most thorough surveys of witchcraft and Pagan traditions in the United States currently available. Much of it is outdated, but it still serves as a solid orientation to some of the most prominent forms of contemporary witchcraft (and surrounding traditions).

The Triumph of the Moon: A History of Modern Pagan Witchcraft, 2nd edition, by Ronald Hutton (Oxford: Oxford University Press, 2019)
The most comprehensive examination of the development of witchcraft as a contemporary religion currently available. This book covers the major players, the most significant influences, and the ways in which some of the most prominent traditions of witchcraft have shifted and grown in the twentieth century and beyond.

Pagan Religions in 5 Minutes, edited by Suzanne Owen and Angela Puca (Sheffield, UK: Equinox, 2024)
Not exclusively about witchcraft, this accessible text is designed to answer many of the most common questions about Paganism, magic, and witchcraft through short essays written by leading scholars working on these subjects.

From Witches

Each of these books presents witchcraft in a distinct way—as religion, as practice, as a deeply personal journey of self-discovery, and more—from a different individual or cultural perspective. Reading several introductory books quickly reveals that there is no singular, representative witchcraft.

Mexican Sorcery: A Practical Guide to Brujeria de Rancho by Laura Davila (Newburyport, MA: Weiser, 2023)

The Dabbler's Guide to Witchcraft: Seeking an Intentional Magical Path by Fire Lyte (New York: Simon Element, 2021)

Initiated: Memoir of a Witch by Amanda Yates Garcia (New York: Grand Central Publishing, 2019)

Waking the Witch: Reflections on Women, Magic, and Power by Pam Grossman (New York: Gallery Books, 2019)

Modern Witch: Spells, Recipes & Workings by Devin Hunter (Woodbury, MN: Llewellyn, 2020)

Brujas: The Magic and Power of Witches of Color by Lorraine Monteagut (Chicago: Chicago Review Press, 2022)

Witchbody: A Graphic Novel by Sabrina Scott (Newburyport, MA: Weiser, 2019)

Enchantments: A Modern Witch's Guide to Self-Possession by Mya Spalter (New York: Dial Press, 2022)

A Spell in the Wild: A Year (and Six Centuries) of Magic by Alice Tarbuck (London: Two Roads, 2020)

Chapter 2

Witchcraft in Context

We've already seen how tricky it can be to pin down exactly what witchcraft is, as well as who practices it. Witchcraft exists in a nebulous web of interconnected ideas, religious traditions, social movements, and the vocabulary of many communities, each of which is full of sometimes very different people. In this chapter, we'll take the time to parse some of that web. Before we get to the specifics of how witches practice magic, what beliefs they hold, and what sorts of things they're doing in their rituals, we need to equip ourselves with some terms and a little bit of history. Witch, Wiccan, Pagan, Neo-Pagan, and New Age are all words that are sometimes used interchangeably, and there's enough overlap between all of these (and more!) that it's worth taking a look at why and how these are conflated and where they depart in significant ways.

We'll start by briefly taking a closer look at Wicca, one of the most widespread traditions of witchcraft, and what separates it from other types that you might encounter. No one appreciates being miscategorized, and the non-Wiccan witches in your life will appreciate not being lumped in with a tradition they don't practice simply because it is often the only variety outsiders get to hear about, so it's best to clear up that confusion early! We'll also discuss the relationship between witchcraft and contemporary Paganism. A great number of witches also identify as Pagans, and the Pagan movement has been instrumental in the rise of witchcraft, though, again, there are divergences that are important for many of today's practitioners. Finally, we'll consider some of the adjacent religious traditions and movements that have been combined with witchcraft, have influenced witchcraft, and continue to overlap with witchcraft communities today, including the New Age, Spiritualism, New Thought, and Theosophy.

Separating Wicca and Witchcraft

One of the great difficulties of exploring witchcraft for the first time and getting the lay of the land in witchcraft communities is navigating the vocabulary. In the previous chapter, we discussed how witches might conceive of their traditions and practices as religion, as spirituality, as practice, and as identity. These are useful categories for thinking about how witchcraft might fit into the cultural and religious landscape and for explaining how so many perspectives can exist under the same umbrella, but they may not be immediately useful faced with the whirling storm of vocabulary that is sure to hit you in your initial forays. Scholars of religion, anthropologists, and sociologists today (as well as an assortment of government officials, journalists, and online content creators) are likely to use a number of key phrases in describing witchcraft: new religious movement, New Age, metaphysical, Neo-Pagan, magical, paranormal, and potentially more. Before we dive into these, let's start with a deceptively tricky distinction that plagues both beginner witches and outsiders alike: Wicca and witchcraft.

The story of Wicca begins with Gerald Gardner (1884–1964), a British customs officer who spent much of his youth in Madeira, Sri Lanka (formerly Ceylon), and Malaysia. Largely self-educated—according to his own telling, even teaching himself to read—and famously eccentric, Gardner was deeply interested in folklore and anthropology. Late in life, Gardner claimed to have been initiated into a secret witchcraft tradition in England's New Forest. Influenced by the popular anthropology of the day, as well as a general disillusionment spurred by industrialization, World War II, and a frustration with mainstream religion, Gardner and his followers believed that witchcraft was a pre-Christian survival of an indigenous European religion, driven underground by Christian persecution. Gardner would publish several books about the witch cult, which he described as highly secretive, only passing its beliefs and traditions through initiatory rites or within close families. These included the worship of a goddess of the moon, a god of death and resurrection, an emphasis on reincarnation, the observance of seasonal rites tied to the fertility of the land, and also the practice of magic. By the last quarter of the twentieth century, this system of witchcraft had coalesced into what we now call Wicca.

The vast majority of Wiccans understand their tradition to be religious and maintain recognizable beliefs and practices that make it distinct among other kinds of witchcraft. Which of those specific beliefs and practices are the most important and most defining is a matter of debate for Wiccans themselves. Some point to the worship of the goddess and god (sometimes a specific goddess and god and other times a variety of potentially interchangeable goddesses and gods that may change according to circumstance), who are seen as embodied in the moon and in the seasonal cycles of the earth. Others point to specific ritual structures, including the use of a magic circle inscribed by the practitioner and then divided into quarters through the invocation of four elemental spirits: earth, air, fire, and water. These four elements are also represented in a specific set of tools that are typical in Wiccan ritual: a chalice or cup, a wand, a special black-handled knife called an athame, and an inscribed disc called a pentacle. Some also point to a particular set of magical admonitions that many Wiccans use both to inform their ritual practice, and also their moral decisions. The most famous of these is what has come to be called the Wiccan Rede, a short aphorism that is often thought to comprise Wicca's central ethical code: "An' it harm none, do as ye will." This is often shortened to the pithy "harm none" and variously interpreted to mean that Wiccans should not practice negative magic or otherwise engage in harmful behaviors. The Wiccan Rede is often accompanied by another tenet called the Law of Three, or sometimes the Law of Threefold Return, which advises that one's actions return threefold (thus, good actions are encouraged and negative ones spurned).

The reality, however, is that Wicca is decentralized, varies by region, includes a number of different traditions, and has shifted dramatically between its mid-twentieth century inception and today. No single statement above universally applies to every witch who identifies as Wiccan, let alone all of them at once. Furthermore, the descriptions of Wicca developed by outsiders (including other sorts of witches) are often oversimplified or incomplete. The Wiccan Rede, for example, becomes ubiquitous relatively late in Wicca's development and is never adopted universally, so we can hardly assert that it is the defining feature. In the coming chapters, we'll discuss in greater detail what Wiccans and other sorts of witches believe, and also what they're actually doing. For now, though, it is important to understand that this distinction is important to practitioners on both sides, especially as non-Wiccan forms of witchcraft come to the fore and increasingly take up more space and where these practitioners seem to increasingly outnumber Wiccans. Though the terms are sometimes used interchangeably—especially by some scholars and other sorts of outsiders, and by some practitioners within particular contexts—Wicca does not define the entire contemporary witchcraft movement. The reason so many people think it does, however, is because Wicca is long-standing, highly visible, and popular with many practitioners. Because of its prominence, it is often the first tradition that new witches explore, and its role as a focal point for various kinds of popular media has ensured that many of Wicca's unique structures, tenets, and texts have made their way into the common parlance of magical and metaphysical spaces more widely. Wicca is as diverse and varied as other traditions of witchcraft, but the direct tie to the work of Gerald Gardner makes it distinct.[7]

Related Movements

Because witchcraft itself is arguably not a singular movement with one shared trajectory, it is critical to consider it within the context of a number of other traditions that flourished at around

7. We will learn more about the story of Gardner and the wider influence of Wicca in chapter 3.

the same time and just before witchcraft came to the fore in the public imagination. None of us exists in a vacuum, and sometimes in the retelling of our various personal narratives it is easy to lose sight of our own beginnings, simply pointing to vague and dubious antiquity or trusting that the family traditions we've inherited are original and unique rather than equally the amalgamations of the popular ideas floating around during our ancestors' time. Sometimes that cherished cookie recipe passed down in the family cookbook is truly original, but more often than not it was initially copied from elsewhere, the origins forgotten. This was the case with my own inherited secret favorite, which with the tiniest bit of research turned out to be the Nestlé Toll House recipe originally published in 1939, lightly modified with personal touches by succeeding family bakers. In many ways, witchcraft is much the same. As creative and personal as it is, and as much as it may point to a distant past, contemporary witchcraft is also very clearly the relative of a number of modern movements, either developing directly within and alongside them or borrowing extensively from them in the form of ideas, specific practices, and vocabulary. Here, we meet some of the most significant influences on witchcraft.

New Thought

Most scholars begin the story of New Thought with New Hampshire–based clockmaker Phineas Quimby (1802–1866). Struggling with his own illness, Quimby witnessed a healing demonstration from itinerant mesmerist Charles Poyen in 1838 and became a believer in the power of the mind to cure. Experimenting on himself (apparently with success!), Quimby also began to travel to give demonstrations as well as to take on students (including Mary Baker Eddy, who would go on to become the founder of the related movement, Christian Science). Quimby taught that disease took hold in the body through the presence of incorrect thoughts, and that by changing one's thinking one could be cured. For Quimby, many of those incorrect thoughts originated in the Christian fear of damnation, and he saw his own practice as a kind of spiritual science, which was itself a revelation from God. The task for humanity, then, became the refinement of one's thoughts for the purpose of unification with what came to be called the "Divine Mind"—a phrase that we still encounter in witchcraft and many forms of contemporary spirituality.[8]

New Thought was codified largely by Quimby's students and admirers, some of them bringing these ideas into more overtly religious spaces, and others venturing into the realms of psychology. One of those intellectual descendants was William Walker Atkinson, who authored a number of books on the subject and often gets credit for the anonymously published *The Kybalion: A Study of the Hermetic Philosophy of Ancient Egypt and Greece* (1908). *The Kybalion*—which claims continuity with ancient wisdom—teaches a series of metaphysical principles that have been and continue to be enormously influential in magical spaces, even where that influence may not be known or acknowledged. These principles include the principle of vibration, which states, "Every thought, emotion or mental state has its corresponding rate and mode of vibration. And by an effort of the will of the person . . . these mental states may be reproduced, just as a musical

8. Beryl Satter, *Each Mind a Kingdom: American Women, Sexual Purity, and the New Thought Movement, 1875–1920* (Berkeley: University of California Press, 1999), 57–62.

tone may be reproduced by causing an instrument to vibrate at a certain rate—just as color may be reproduced in the same way."[9] If you've ever thought that someone had "bad vibes" or heard that objects (like crystals) possess "vibrations" that can impact their surroundings, you can in part thank the authors of the New Thought movement!

Of all of the related traditions we will explore, New Thought may be one of the least familiar, but this movement has had a great deal of influence on many things that we take for granted in everyday life. If you've ever been told that thinking positively could make good things come your way, that you could cure illness through visualizing yourself healthy, or that you could manifest your desires by intentionally imagining them, you've probably been tangentially touched by New Thought. It's been particularly impactful in the realm of contemporary witchcraft. Many of the ideas that we today associate with self-help and productivity have their roots in this nineteenth and twentieth century new religious movement, and most of us don't think of them as religious at all—they're so integrated into our cultural landscape. They're part of corporate life, hustle culture, and a wide variety of religious and spiritual traditions.

New Thought has been cemented into the mainstream though a number of channels, including Alcoholics Anonymous, the popularity of media personality Oprah Winfrey, the Prosperity Gospel as preached by televangelists like Joel Osteen, and the Human Potential Movement, which has impacted much of the theory behind professional development that is popular in

9. Three Initiates, *The Kybalion: Centenary Edition* (New York: TarcherPerigee, 2018), 92.

corporate settings today. The New Thought movement has also bestowed many significant books upon today's readers, including the 2007 bestseller *The Secret* by Rhonda Byrne. Both the Law of Attraction—the principle that "like attracts like"—and the popular practice of manifestation find their roots in New Thought, making their way into many forms of contemporary witchcraft via the New Age, popular culture, or directly though texts like *The Kybalion*.[10]

Spiritualism

The end of the nineteenth century was something of a turning point for mysticism, magic, and the supposed powers of the mind in the American religious landscape. Around the same time that Quimby and other proponents of the "mind cure movement" of New Thought were traveling, teaching, writing, and cultivating their ideas into fruition, another influential movement was also being born: Spiritualism. In 1848 in Hydesville, NY, sisters Catherine and Margaretta Fox reported hearing a ghostly rapping in the home they shared with their parents, which the family had determined was being made by the spirit of a murdered

10. My own introduction to *The Kybalion* came courtesy of my very first visit to a metaphysical supply store in Northern Virginia, as a teenager curious about Wicca. The store carried witchcraft supplies, magical books, tarot decks, and more, and when I asked the owner for a recommendation (I had read most of the material normally recommended to beginners at that point), she handed me *The Kybalion*, with the caveat that, though it was essential reading, its message might be "too much" for me at this early stage. I wouldn't read it in full until several years later, while studying with a coven that used it as a teaching tool.

man buried in their cellar.[11] Over time, the girls developed a system for communicating with this spirit (and others as well) and began to give public demonstrations that captured the imaginations of people all over New York and beyond. Many people—especially women, who held significant positions as leaders in the Spiritualism movement—learned the art of mediumship and worked with bereaved and curious clients alike to communicate with lost loved ones.

Spiritualism became a religious movement all its own, with many staunch and vocal advocates among the middle and upper classes. Spiritualism believers formed churches and organized countryside retreats called camps (the most famous of which is in Lily Dale, NY) where attendees could participate in séances and attend lectures. In many ways, the climate was ripe for such a movement. The American Civil War (1861–1865) had been shockingly catastrophic, leaving well over half a million dead and far from home, their remaining families anxious for any kind of final reunion. An intricate Victorian mourning culture also served as backdrop, featuring the development and popularity of many sentimental practices (for example, particular styles of black attire, death photography, and various kinds of mourning jewelry containing things like woven hair from the deceased) that

11. No corpse was found, though rumors still circulate, and only the house's original foundation remains. It is now a popular "haunted" destination for tourists determined to hear the mysterious rappings for themselves. The young women's older sister, Leah, was apparently of the opinion that the younger girls were less than honest about the source of the rappings, and Margaretta would publicly confess to the fraud in 1888 (only to recant the confession a year later!). You can find an accessible and engaging retelling of their story in Barbara Weisberg's *Talking to the Dead: Kate and Maggie Fox and the Rise of Spiritualism* (New York: HarperCollins, 2004).

recentered the focus from the dead to the survivors themselves.[12] That so many during this period, in both the United States and Europe, were keen to assert that their lost loved ones could still interact with the living should perhaps not be surprising. What's more, Spiritualism did not exclusively use the language of faith or belief. Instead, practitioners were invited to think of themselves as investigators and even scientists, testing their techniques, collecting evidence, and comparing results with their fellows. Spiritualism promised an afterlife comparable to the world of the living, in many ways normalizing the impact of death and troubling the boundary between our worlds. Antiauthoritarian and non-hierarchical, it also rejected many other binaries, including the divide between men and women. Spiritualism offered a space in which gender need not define one's access to authority, and indeed many of Spiritualism's most prominent leaders have been and still are women.

Though you may be less likely to meet as many people today who identify explicitly as Spiritualists (though there are still Spiritualist churches all over the world!), the ideas, techniques, and vocabulary of Spiritualism are a part of the everyday parlance of witches and other sorts of magically minded folks. Many witches identify as mediums, engage in séances, and think of communication with the dead as core to the practice of witchcraft. Many of these associations are less to do with any particular history of witches and are instead directly tied to the popularity of Spiritualism in the United States and parts of Europe, which hasn't so much waned as it has been reshaped into a collective passion

12. Molly McGarry, *Ghosts of Futures Past: Spiritualism and the Cultural Politics of Nineteenth-Century America* (Berkeley: University of California Press, 2008), 8–9.

for the paranormal. The popularity of ghost hunting television shows, ghost tours (indeed, a whole paranormal tourism industry), tales of hauntings, paranormal conventions, and the glut of ghost hunting accoutrements available from a variety of retailers can all trace some of their roots to Spiritualism and early efforts in the adjacent field of parapsychology. This investment in ghosts, ghost hunting, and the afterlife has led to a number of borrowings by contemporary witches. The concept and terminology surrounding spirit guides comes to us via Spiritualism, as do many popular divination techniques, including the use of talking boards and pendulums. The practices of channeling and automatic writing also come to witchcraft via Spiritualism, as well as the conception of the afterlife as "the Summerland," a phrase popular in Wicca and some other kinds of witchcraft. The assertion, too, that the magical practices of witchcraft are akin to a science and not religion at all also echoes the early Spiritualists.

Theosophy

The Theosophical Society was founded in New York in 1875 by a group of scholars and mystics that took for their central mission the establishment of a universal doctrine that could unite humankind as one brotherhood through the study of the world's esoteric wisdom. Led by Helena Blavatsky, Henry Steel Olcott, and William Quan Judge, the Theosophical Society described itself as non-sectarian and even as a scientific community bent on the discovery of universal truth through both the comparative study of religion and also investigations into what we today might call the paranormal. The headquarters of the Theosophical Society would move to India in 1882, where it would be heavily involved in the translation and distribution of a number of sacred texts, cementing for many Westerners the idea that the East is inherently a bastion of mysticism and spirituality.[13] In 1907, British activist Annie Besant would become the president of the Theosophical Society, and her prolific body of writing remains heavily influential in a number of esoteric spaces.

One of the central teachings of these early Theosophists was that the world's religions fundamentally pointed to a shared universal wisdom that transcended any singular system. By studying the ancient traditions of the world, we can locate the truth behind the laws of nature and transcend the base materialism plaguing society. This universal wisdom is transmitted to humanity through the teachings of what Blavatsky called Mahatmas, and what subsequently were called Ascended Masters. These were adepts—evolved human beings who underwent multiple incarnations and spiritual initiations in order to bestow humanity with the lessons required to collectively grow and enter a more enlightened state of being. According to Blavatsky, these great teachers include Jesus, Krishna, Buddha, and more (other Theosophists pointed to many such teachers, accessed through the practice of channeling).

Though the Theosophical Society is still active today, its presence among today's witches is outwardly minimal. In fact, you are much more likely to hear contemporary witches criticizing both Blavatsky directly and Theosophy as a whole as fundamentally appropriative and responsible for the whitewashing of a number of traditions, the consequences of which are still impacting how Americans and Europeans portray and understand many forms

13. Alex Owen, *The Place of Enchantment: British Occultism and the Culture of the Modern* (Chicago: University of Chicago Press, 2004), 31.

of Buddhism and Hinduism today. Despite these critiques, however, the influence of Theosophy within witchcraft communities remains substantial, if at times invisible. It shines through in many popular attitudes about reincarnation, as well as in the way many witches describe the concept of karma, which has been borrowed widely in the West. It also lends us the language of the "astral plane," an adjacent, invisible realm where many witches assert that magic takes place (you may have heard of "astral projection," in which someone sends their consciousness out of their body to view things either far away or in other realms of existence). Many of the healing modalities and spiritual frameworks that witches sometimes incorporate (and which many are seeking to decolonize as we collectively become more conscious of the impact of cultural appropriation and white supremacy) are not inherited directly from their original systems, but rather were filtered through the lens of Theosophy.[14] Some of our popular assumptions about the universality of religion also find roots in Theosophy.

The New Age

It is very difficult to pinpoint the beginning of the New Age movement or even to say exactly where its boundaries are. We could begin in potentially a number of places and find it relatively easy to observe continuity with older movements. Most scholars point to the counterculture of the 1960s and 1970s, whose tumul-

14. Examples of this include some kinds of yoga and also the concept of energy centers in the body called chakras. Both yoga and the chakra system have lengthy and deep histories within their originating traditions of Hinduism but shifted (in some cases quite substantially) via their distribution in the West through the Theosophical Society.

tuous political climate created an environment where antiauthoritarianism ruled. Amid the American Civil Rights Movement and protests against the Vietnam War came a sexual revolution, a widespread interest in psychedelic drugs, rock and roll, environmentalism, and various alternative lifestyles. All this political and creative upheaval impacted many religious communities as well, and young people in particular, disaffected by the mainstream, sought other avenues of spiritual exploration. An interest in a variety of Asian religious and spiritual traditions flourished, as well as a fascination with Indigenous American cultures and practices. These were combined in an eclectic mix, along with the strands of older movements like New Thought, Spiritualism, and Theosophy to create a bricolage of personal practices that could be tailored to each individual.

Characteristic of the New Age is a deep investment in both personal and societal transformation, hence the term—we are either arriving in a New Age of personal being or ushering in a New Age for humanity collectively. Practitioners engage in a number of activities that center both physical and emotional healing and also self-knowledge. Often, these are framed in terms of ascending to higher states of consciousness, uniting or reuniting with a kind of divine essence, or achieving a state of universal wisdom that in turn helps the entirety of humankind likewise ascend, heal, or otherwise transform. These practices include various kinds of energetic healing systems like reiki, meditation, visualization, past-life regression, channeling, crystal healing, manifestation, tarot card reading, astrology, and psychic development. The New Age tends to emphasize interconnectedness and holistic thinking, which leads to blurring between the sacred and the mundane. Potentially anything can take on cosmic significance, as the divine exists both within us and in the world around us. Rather than organizing into structured groups, New Age practitioners tend to prefer specialist-client or student-teacher relationships. Experts (like tarot readers or energy healers) share their services with paying clients, and various types of knowledge may be acquired through things like correspondence courses, workshops, and conferences.[15]

One of the most curious and difficult things about analyzing the New Age as a collective movement is that, today, the terms "New Age" and "New Ager" are often used pejoratively to imply that a practitioner, group, or idea is somehow inauthentic, appropriative, shallow, or unsound. This is especially true among witches. When the objective of some types of witchcraft is to connect with the past and assert continuity with older cultures and magical systems, implying that something is New Age (or new at all) is sometimes construed as an insult. This is especially true as the New Age is increasingly associated with cultural appropriation, whitewashing traditional historical practices, and indiscriminately and carelessly blending conflicting practices. Whereas in previous decades the term "New Age" may have been more neutral, today it is frequently dismissive. Even practitioners who fit our definitions and partake in these narratives and histories are unlikely to actually identify as New Age. Instead, you are more likely to encounter the terms "spirituality," "mind-body-spirit," or "Aquarian" or else to hear other traditions or categories named (for example, practitioners may identify as shamans, as

15. Sarah Pike, *New Age and Neopagan Religions in America* (New York: Columbia University Press, 2004), 23.

witches, as mystics, as occultists, as spiritual but not religious, or simply as spiritual). They may engage in New Age practices and share a belief in the need for personal or societal spiritual transformation without actually identifying as New Age. Increasingly, this is a term that belongs to outsiders and is *applied* to others rather than claimed and embraced by a recognizably distinct community of practitioners.

In some ways, the New Age is as much a genre, a social perspective, and a consumer market as it is a distinct religious movement. As a market, the New Age is characterized by eclecticism and an interest in the religious practices of world cultures (particularly Asian and Indigenous American traditions) and especially in the desire to make those practices universally applicable and transferable. New Age literature is as much a part of the self-help genre as it is overtly religious, and New Age perspectives often make their way into health and healing, business, psychology, and productivity culture. All of these also overlap with witchcraft, sometimes making the two movements impossible to totally separate. Witches are likely to pull from the New Age freely, to use similar language and tools, and to share many of the same spaces.

Paganism

Like the New Age, Paganism is difficult to parse as a singular new religious movement because it includes a number of very different traditions, each with their own unique histories. It is an umbrella term that potentially encompasses everything from some kinds of witchcraft, to reconstructed polytheistic traditions, to feminist Goddess worshippers, to several Western esoteric traditions, to the newly constructed spiritual traditions inspired by pop culture and personal gnosis that intrepid practitioners might openly create and expand upon individually. There is no central organizing body, no common ethic, no universal practice, and no singular historical narrative that people who identify as Pagans (or who simply get called Pagans) inherently share. Along with the New Age, many scholars place the inception of the Neo-Pagan movement with the 1960s counterculture, pointing to the same trends that we've discussed above, but in some cases groups that we might construe as Pagan had existed somewhat earlier (like Wicca and some strands of contemporary Druidry). Some scholars point to the founding of the Church of All Worlds in the United States in 1967, and indeed, founder Oberon Zell often gets credit for coining the term "Neo-Pagan" and being the first to publicly claim "Pagan" as a religious identity.[16]

Defining characteristics of Paganism tend to include the sacralization of nature and a cosmology that places the divine in the natural world. Practitioners tend to celebrate holy days around the changing seasons and to prefer engaging in these celebrations outdoors or otherwise in natural spaces instead of constructing designated buildings like churches or temples. They engage in various kinds of rituals—often creative, fluid acts of pageantry that pull from many sources—that tend to center personal transformation and healing. Pagans also tend to prioritize looking to the past, drawing inspiration from and sometimes claiming continuity with pre-Christian traditions. Many Pagans assert that their practices are not new at all, but rather that they are members of the "old religion." Sometimes the term "Pagan"

16. John C. Sulak, *The Wizard and the Witch: Seven Decades of Counterculture, Magick & Paganism* (Woodbury, MN: Llewellyn Publications, 2014), 49.

is used playfully or provocatively, to denote that the user exists outside of the mainstream as defined by Christianity and may or may not see themselves as part of a cohesive religious tradition.

One of the troubles with defining Paganism is that we struggle to even refer to it by a singular name. You may hear people describe themselves as Pagan or Neo-Pagan, and scholars are prone to using the phrase "contemporary Pagan," or sometimes (increasingly rarely) the unhyphenated Neopagan. There are very subtle differences between each of these for the practitioners who use them (and sometimes the insistence that one is correct and the others are not is quite vehement). In the same way that "New Age" has become a pejorative, sometimes "Neo-Pagan" is flung to imply that a person's practice is inauthentic, fabricated, or otherwise too modern (and therefore not to be taken seriously among practitioners who measure authenticity by age).

Many witches are comfortable under the umbrella term "Pagan" and see witchcraft as one expression of this nature-based, polytheistic religious movement. Most Wiccan witches identify as Pagans, and Wicca usually fits neatly into the histories scholars tell of the development of Paganism as a contemporary religious movement, especially in the United States. Wicca is nature-based in the sense that it celebrates seasonal cycles and tends to see the divine as manifested in the natural world, and Wicca is also typically polytheistic (individual Wiccans may interpret their deities through a variety of lenses and may use a variety of terms). Other sorts of witches also may identify as Pagans, especially those who also place spiritual significance on the cycles of nature. "Pagan" is also sometimes used interchangeably with "polytheist," so witches who worship or work with particular deities within a polytheistic framework are also likely to use the term. Sometimes, polytheists describe their particular cosmologies as "hard polytheism" or "soft polytheism." In the former, deities may be conceived of as distinct, separate, and self-contained with their own unique modes of worship and individual preferences. In the latter, they are potentially conflatable, interchangeable, and fundamentally connected as reflections of a singular divine source. Some polytheists prefer these terms in lieu of Pagan—and especially Neo-Pagan—specifically because they understand their own traditions to be older, culturally specific, and unconnected to the modern movement as defined by most scholars and contemporary Pagan practitioners.

Though witches today do occasionally manage to reliably point to a more distant past, the stamp of the modern is impossible to miss. Our practices and beliefs are a kind of bricolage, even where we may identify with very specific magical traditions and histories. None of us ever totally escapes our cultural environment. Like fish in a bowl, we swim in a mix of ideas and assumptions, as invisible and taken for granted as water. For contemporary witches, that water is the nineteenth- and twentieth-century religious movements we've introduced in this chapter. All the above movements have at times consciously identified directly as occultism and have also been categorized as occult by outsiders. In the most basic sense, the word "occult" simply means hidden or obscured. The word is also used interchangeably to mean esoteric, mystical, or magical, and in this sense witchcraft fits neatly into the category as well. Some practitioners embrace the term—especially those who see witchcraft as fundamentally secretive and exclusive—but others don't because it can sometimes evoke negative associations and doesn't necessarily reflect witchcraft's wide appeal (especially for those practitioners who see witchcraft as an up-and-coming world religion, available to all).

History is a funny thing. Outside of academic spaces, we often talk about history as though it were objective, neat, and devoid of personal biases or ideological agendas, but this simply isn't the case. The truth is that any story we might tell about the development of witchcraft would sound different depending on many variables: when we start, where we place our focus, whom we allow to narrate, and what purpose lies behind the telling. Because there is not one witchcraft, there cannot be one history. Most retellings of the history of contemporary witchcraft, especially those told from Wiccan perspectives, begin with Gerald Gardner and his peers writing, experimenting, and garnering public attention in England and then shortly thereafter in the United States. Other witches begin at other moments. Each of our respective narratives should be approached critically, keeping in mind that the desire to establish authenticity through age sometimes causes us to be too quick to accept dubious evidence. Considering this larger context helps us place witchcraft in a more clearly defined lineage and to make better sense of the many perspectives that you are sure to encounter in witch spaces. The histories we tell (and the histories we deny) as well as the words we choose for ourselves—witch versus Wiccan, Pagan versus Neo-Pagan, occult versus New Age—all potentially carry a great deal of weight for the individual practitioner and require careful attention on the part of outsiders in order to fully understand and respect.

Suggested Reading

From Scholars

New Age and Neopagan Religions in America by Sarah Pike (New York: Columbia University Press, 2004)

This is a relatively short and highly accessible survey of Neopaganism and the New Age in the United States, both of which potentially include contemporary witchcraft. Pike's work is especially helpful for thinking about how these movements overlap and where they fit in a wider study of American religions.

The Place of Enchantment: British Occultism and the Culture of the Modern by Alex Owen (Chicago: University of Chicago Press, 2004)

A comprehensive exploration of the esoteric currents that form the modern occult movement. Owen's work is invaluable in any consideration of the relationship between the magical and modernity. Though the book is not explicitly about witchcraft, many of the people and traditions Owen presents are those largely responsible for how and why witchcraft looks the way it does today.

Madame Blavatsky's Baboon: A History of the Mystics, Mediums, and Misfits Who Brought Spiritualism to America by Peter Washington (New York: Schocken Books, 1993)

An approachable and at times very funny general history of the movements that would eventually give us the New Age.

From Witches

Each of these books was originally released several decades ago and is widely considered a classic in contemporary witch spaces.

All are good illustrations of how witchcraft often includes and reflects a variety of religious perspectives and historical movements, combined and recombined in ways that might be invisible to practitioners of later generations.

Wicca: A Comprehensive Guide to the Old Religion in the Modern World by Vivianne Crowley (London: Element, 2003)

Power of the Witch by Laurie Cabot with Tom Cowan (New York: Delta, 1989)

Mastering Witchcraft: A Practical Guide for Witches, Warlocks & Covens by Paul Huson (New York: Putnam, 1970)

The Inner Temple of Witchcraft by Christopher Penczak, 20th anniv. ed. (Woodbury, MN: Llewellyn, 2021)

Witchcraft for Tomorrow by Doreen Valiente (London: Hale Books, 1978)

Positive Magic: A Toolkit for the Modern Witch by Marion Weinstein (Newburyport, MA: Weiser, 2020)

Chapter 3

Many Types of Witchcraft

A cursory exploration of witchcraft on social media will reveal the staggering variety of descriptions and monikers that witches today use to label both their individual identities and also their magical practices. You may have already encountered some of these. Some of the more common varieties—Wicca, traditional witchcraft, Feri, Reclaiming, green witchcraft, eclectic witchcraft—adorn the spines of books and have entire social media hubs devoted to them. Others are more obscure, either existing within particular community pockets or else only recently gaining traction outside of their niches—folk witchcraft, secular witchcraft, cosmic witchcraft, Luciferian witchcraft, and dozens more besides. This seemingly endless assortment can be overwhelming and is one of the most bewildering parts of exploring witchcraft for anyone who chooses to do so. Are all these just variations of the same tradition? Are these the equivalent of denominations? How do all these kinds of witches coexist, or do they? How do you interact with practitioners and learn more without accidentally being dismissive or offensive?

The way that we categorize witchcraft has shifted dramatically in recent decades. This is true both from scholarly perspectives and from witches themselves. In previous chapters, we discussed the many definitions of witchcraft that exist, and for the purposes of this book we made a distinction between historical witchcraft—the witchcraft described by medieval, early modern, and colonial American historians, as well as the witchcraft documented in witch hunt trial records—and the contemporary witchcraft that people today practice. It's important to understand, though, that this distinction is somewhat arbitrary. I'm making it for the sake of clarity and convenience in a book designed to help readers understand how witches today live and think of their own traditions and practices, not because contemporary and historical practices are inherently distinct. There are many witches today who understand their witchcraft to be directly descendant from those described in the documentation of European witch persecutions. Many more understand their traditions as continuations of ancestral practices, whether in an unbroken lineage or as reclamations or reconstructions. For them, my distinction is a false one. Their own boundaries and taxonomies would be different and perhaps based on things that would seem false to me.

This difference discredits neither of us. Rather, it serves as a reminder that our labels are flexible, movable, and shift depending on who we are, what our agendas are, and the contexts in which we are surrounded. I started this book with a bracket around contemporary witchcraft because I wanted to clarify to readers that this is not about history. My goal is to familiarize you with how witches practice today. That doesn't mean that historians, folklorists, and witches themselves can't or haven't made connections to historical witchcraft, but when we're creating taxonomies, we need both a beginning and an end point. Where those are is rarely permanently fixed.

This flexible perspective is critical for navigating the constantly growing and changing landscape of witchcraft types and traditions. It allows us to understand how new types are created, why individual witches might describe themselves with different labels in different environments or at different times in their lives, why there often appears to be so much overlap, and why we sometimes find such stark differences across generations of witches. Sometimes the monikers and descriptions that witches use point to clear delineations of practice and belief, but just as often they are about feeling, preference, or the individual need to affirm one's own identity. All these distinctions are valid and important, but they also guarantee that we will never run out of new categories and that witches as a whole will never collectively agree with every boundary. I could provide you with an exhaustive list of types and traditions, complete with definitions and detailed histories, and it would be woefully outdated in only a handful of years. Witches tend to prioritize personal authority and individual exploration, which means that change happens quickly in witchcraft communities. Instead of trying to master lists of traditions or struggling to build a more complete taxonomy, it's often better to look for larger patterns across groups of practitioners, and to get comfortable simply asking the witches in your life what they mean by their own descriptors for themselves.

In this chapter, we'll take a look at some of these larger patterns and themes you're sure to encounter. What follows is a framework you can use for beginning to situate the many kinds of witchcraft, though it's important to remember that many witches won't fit neatly into any single group (and lots will fit into more than one).

The Influence of Wicca

Wicca, as we've learned, is one form of witchcraft among many. Its origins and influences are traceable and have been well-documented by scholars in recent decades, and while it's true that many early practitioners erroneously believed the religion to be a survival of an indigenous European tradition, the overwhelming majority of Wiccans publishing and speaking today embrace its modernity. For many Wiccan witches, Wicca's modernity is part of its appeal. Its comparative youth makes it flexible and expansive, with individual practitioners often encouraged to experiment and modify it to suit their personal needs and perspectives. Like many other religious traditions, Wicca has developed into a number of varieties since its beginning, with some practitioners adhering closely to the tradition as it was initially practiced by Gerald Gardner and his contemporaries and others expanding and diverging into forms that might seem related in name alone.

Traditional Wicca

Some Wiccan traditions, like Gardnerian Wicca and Alexandrian Wicca, resemble the fraternal orders and secret societies that influenced and inspired their founders, including Freemasonry, the Hermetic Order of the Golden Dawn, and the Ordo Templi Orientis. This variety of Wicca is sometimes called traditional

Wicca, British Traditional Wicca, or initiatory Wicca. Members organize themselves into groups called covens, normally under the leadership of a high priestess or some other elder of sufficient rank and experience. These groups tend to be hierarchical, with members participating in a degree system designating authority within the coven. Newcomers become members via some sort of initiation ritual, undertaking an oath to preserve the secret nature of the tradition and the rites practiced by the coven. Most traditional Wiccan groups emphasize an initiatory lineage connecting practitioners through a magical line, back to the tradition's founders in a kind of family tree. Individual covens tend to be autonomous—not answering to any kind of official governing body—but recognize members of the tradition through their place in this initiatory lineage. As traditional Wicca has developed and grown, it has split into a wide variety of traditions, many with very different beliefs and ritual practices. Even within the oldest forms of traditional Wicca a great deal of variety exists, though many assert unbroken consistency with Gerald Gardner and the earliest Wiccan covens.

Other traditions have sprung up and taken root without formal connections to an initiatory lineage, sometimes founded by practitioners who have left their original groups or else by witches who have been inspired by books and have assembled new traditions based on initiatory models. In this way, Wicca closely resembles the denominational models that are familiar to so many through Christianity. We might call it an organized religion, though that level of organization is often quite loose. As you could probably guess, there is no shortage of internal conflict related to belonging, authority, and correct belief and practice.

Not all initiated Wiccans recognize each other as valid members, and sometimes traditions split due to contentious disagreements.

Eclectic Wicca

Though the earliest forms of Wicca were initiatory, group-based, and hierarchical, most Wiccans practicing today (and indeed, since publishing spurred Wicca's popularity) adhere to other models entirely. What came to be called "eclectic" Wicca grew to prominence in the last decades of the twentieth century in the United States, articulating a trend in witchcraft spaces that had been brewing since Wiccan witchcraft became a favorite media topic. Lineaged, initiatory covens simply could not accommodate this influx of newcomers interested in becoming witches. And some newcomers had no interest in joining groups at all, more attracted to the image of the witch as a loner (and certainly plenty of historical and cultural precedent exists for this!). Wiccan authors like Doreen Valiente, Ray Buckland, Scott Cunningham, and more published books designed to teach readers to practice Wiccan witchcraft alone, without the need for initiation or training in a coven.[17] In only a few short years many other authors would rise to prominence, advocating not just for solitary Wicca but also for a creative, self-guided, intuitive approach that entailed experimenting with practices and perspectives from

17. It's worth noting that some of the earliest witchcraft writers that were involved in Gerald Gardner's tradition, including Doreen Valiente and Gardner himself, largely did not use the term "Wiccan" to describe themselves, as Wicca was not widely understood to be an inherently distinct flavor of witchcraft at the time. Therefore, calling them "Wiccan" today might be somewhat anachronistic, especially when we consider that some, like Valiente, participated in other systems that today we would consider very distinct.

other religions or magical traditions, keeping what was most appealing and effective and leaving the rest. Authors like Silver RavenWolf, DJ Conway, and Patricia Telesco helped define this approach as "eclecticism," and the term stuck. Eclectic Wicca was accessible in a way that traditional Wicca was not. Eclectic styles of Wicca dominated publishing and the internet, and some even codified into their own traditions over time, adopting initiatory models and developing into large networks of covens and teachers.

Some eclectic Wiccans and solitary Wiccans made substantial changes to the Wicca that had been originally articulated in mid-twentieth century England. Some included new ritual practices or specified ethical codes that were absent from traditional, initiatory Wicca. Some added cultural elements or religious practices from other regions and peoples: for example, deities or cosmologies that were not a component of earlier forms.[18] Some eliminated elements of initiatory Wicca that they deemed distasteful or outdated, such as the hierarchical coven or the practice of ritual nudity. Today, many Wiccan witches have dropped additional labels like "eclectic" or "British traditional," whether out of ease or disfavor. The term "Wicca" includes enormous variety (and plenty of debate surrounding who should or shouldn't use it), and it is difficult even for insiders to point to and agree upon what is "actually Wicca" and what isn't.

Even though the term "eclecticism" developed later, the reality is that Wiccan witchcraft has always been what we might call

18. Sometimes these additions were relatively benign, but this has also led to harmful acts of cultural appropriation. Practitioners today are increasingly conscious of and concerned about cultural appropriation, and many are actively seeking to deconstruct appropriated practices.

"eclectic." Gerald Gardner, Doreen Valiente, and other early Wiccan founders and teachers pulled from a wide array of sources, both European and not, and freely experimented with both magical techniques and spiritual cosmologies. Individual Wiccan covens within the same tradition may have different ritual practices and organizational structures, all while insisting that no change has occurred. This is true today, with marked differences existing, for example, between British and American forms of Gardnerian and Alexandrian Wicca. The result is that any single Wiccan practitioner, tradition, popular book, or social media hub can't possibly be representative of the entirety of Wicca, and what anyone means by the term can sometimes differ drastically.

The early popularity of Wicca and its dominance in publishing in the twentieth century also meant that other forms of witchcraft were largely obscured. In the popular understanding, "Wicca" became synonymous with "witchcraft," and this has heavily impacted witchcraft communities as a whole today. First, it overshadowed the varieties of witchcraft that were different—witchcrafts that belonged to other regions, other peoples, and other times. Wicca may have instigated witchcraft's entry into the popular imagination and the religious landscapes of Britain and the United States, but it has never existed alone, nor has it ever represented the entirety of witchcraft practitioners. Second, Wiccan practices and structures became so ubiquitous that they entered general usage, whether or not incoming practitioners knew their origins. Thus, it's not uncommon for witches today to assert that they are non-Wiccan, though some of their beliefs and practices closely resemble those of Wicca. Sometimes this is due to common magical ancestry—Gerald Gardner was heavily influenced by Western esotericism and British folk traditions, for example—but often it's because of Wicca's earlier monopoly on circulated materials in wider witchcraft and Pagan communities.

Traditional Witchcrafts

Though what we now call Wicca has dominated both in witchcraft spaces and in the popular understanding of contemporary witchcraft, it has never been the only form of witchcraft available to would-be practitioners (especially if we are using a very broad definition of witchcraft that includes folk and ancestral practices that may or may not have widely been considered witchcraft at their respective times). Gerald Gardner had a number of rivals and critics, and during his lifetime and shortly after his death in 1964, other witches would challenge his version of things. Some of these other witches had directly participated in Gardner's system and found it wanting for various reasons, but others purported to belong to older traditions that had been less adulterated by outside influence. There were also movements that developed outside of England that asserted entirely different origins from Wicca altogether, as well as magical, culturally rooted traditions that had been preserved among closed communities pre-dating Wicca's entrance into the public arena.

The Influence of Robert Cochrane

One of the most significant witches directly opposing the more widely publicized witchcraft of the day was Robert Cochrane. Cochrane was not as prolific as Gardner and his cohort—he is known primarily through personal letters and his contributions to witchcraft-related newsletters of the time—but he was charismatic and influential, as were many of the witches he worked with and taught. Cochrane was the leader of another group of witches called the Clan of Tubal Cain and claimed to be a member of a hereditary witchcraft tradition.[19] Cochrane made several objections to how witchcraft was being presented in the media by Gardnerians, including the assertion that it was a form of simple pagan belief tied to human participation in the cycles of nature. Cochrane's writings disparaged the heavily ritualized, celebratory nature of Gardnerian witchcraft.[20] For him, witchcraft was an occult art distinct from paganism, centered upon the mystical pursuit of spiritual knowledge.[21] Cochrane's work was less structured than Wicca (with its heavy grounding in ceremonial magic), and less interested in the worship of specific deities. There are a number of lingering questions surrounding Robert Cochrane and his relationship with Gardnerian Wicca, as well as the legitimacy of his claims to a hereditary tradition (you'll notice that the claim of family connection has been important in a number of forms of witch-

19. A detailed exploration of Cochrane's claims is available via Ronald Hutton, *The Triumph of the Moon*, 2nd ed. (New York: Oxford University Press, 2019), 324–27.
20. Cochrane was also prone to implying that Gardner was only interested in witchcraft for the sake of sexual impropriety, based on the practice of ritual nudity and the ritual use of a small flogger called the scourge. It is important to acknowledge that Gardner was never actually accused of sexual wrongdoing by those who knew him, and the texts produced by those in his covens overwhelmingly describe him in benign, fond terms. Assertions that Gardner committed assorted sexual crimes sometimes circulate in anti-Wiccan witchcraft spaces online, and these are perhaps the result of Cochrane's influence. At the very least, they are not based on the accounts of those who worked with him.
21. Ethan Doyle White, "Robert Cochrane and the Gardnerian Craft," *The Pomegranate: The International Journal of Pagan Studies* 13, no. 2 (2011): 209–10.

craft, some more or less dubious than others), but his influence remains significant regardless.

More important for witches today is the reality that witchcraft is not a singular, unified tradition and never has been. Cochrane, and later writers like Evan John Jones, Michael Howard, and Shani Oates, inspired a number of other practitioners who would go on to define what collectively came to be known as traditional witchcraft, or sometimes "Old Craft." This term by itself is tricky because it has a number of meanings. Some who identify as traditional witches possess a formal ritual connection with Cochrane's tradition, but many more were inspired by his legacy and his distinctly practical approach to witchcraft. Some traditional witches do not point to Cochrane at all and instead make similar claims of connection to their own hereditary traditions. Many traditional witches today are less invested in ancestral claims and instead prioritize the use of practical magic (as opposed to worship or ritual focused on spiritual transformation), which has come to be a hallmark of traditional witch practice. Other traditional witches use the term "non-Wiccan witch" interchangeably, presenting their practice less as a coherent tradition in and of itself and more as a foil to the Wiccan witchcraft that has dominated popular conversations for decades.

One of the most consistently important aspects of traditional witchcraft today is the emphasis on its connection to the land itself and the specific region in which the practitioner lives. Traditional witchcraft includes the folk traditions of the area in which it is located, and this means that it varies as we look at all the different places where it's practiced. A traditional witch in Cornwall or the New Forest is necessarily going to be up to something different than a traditional witch in Appalachia. This doesn't necessarily mean that all traditional witches are only invested in replicating customs from the past. Rather, it means that the witch lives in close communion with the landscape, and their practices are informed by both existing folkways and the cultural shifts that might impact their region. If the witch were to move away, their practice might be very different from one location to the next. Because traditional witchcraft is so dependent on region, there can be quite a lot of variation in the types of magic that any individual witch might employ.

There is also quite a lot of variety in traditional witchcraft cosmologies. Some traditional witches see their traditions as survivals of the historical witchcraft detailed in witch trial literature and folklore, eschewing the contemporary label of "Pagan" that other kinds of witches (especially Wiccan witches) have happily held for decades. Some define their practices as animistic or shamanic, their worlds rich with spirit interactions. Some are theistic, worshipping or working with deities from particular regions and cultures, and others embrace the witch's place in Christian folk traditions as having ties to the Devil and working baneful magic on the outskirts of polite society. Some traditional witches are less interested in any specific religious framework and instead understand their practice to be entirely pragmatic—a collection of techniques and tools designed to magically influence the world according to the individual witch's needs and desires. They may also see their witchcraft as potentially compatible with a variety of distinct religious traditions, mixing their practices with those cosmologies and organizational structures to create a personalized combination.

An American Traditional Witchcraft

Another type of witchcraft that might fall under the broader category of traditional witchcraft is Feri (sometimes called Faery or Anderson Feri). Initiates of Feri assert that the history of their tradition is unrelated to those born in England in the mid-twentieth century and that their teachings and practices predate those of Gerald Gardner and his cohort. Born in 1917 in Clayton, New Mexico, leader Victor Anderson purported to have experienced a magical initiation as a child at the hands of a small old woman who appeared to him as though in a dream.[22] According to his own telling, Anderson subsequently located a surviving coven of witches in Oregon and was initiated into the group in 1932. Anderson and his wife, Cora—who also had a rich magical background thanks to a childhood spent among the folk practices of rural Alabama—would go on to teach their version of witchcraft from their home in California, becoming some of the most influential witches of the day.

Victor Anderson was famous for his reliance on storytelling as a primary component of his teaching strategy, and his students (many of whom subsequently became vocal witchcraft writers and teachers) report that he sometimes provided each of them with different information, reflecting his own shifting and growing relationship with the tradition itself and also an attention to the differing needs of each witch he was training.[23] This flexibility is one of the hallmarks of Feri. Rather than necessarily being beholden to established ritual structures, shared sacred

22. Margot Adler, *Drawing Down the Moon: Witches, Druids, Goddess-Worshippers, and Other Pagans in America Today*, rev. ed. (New York: Penguin, 1986), 78–79.

23. T. Thorn Coyle, *Evolutionary Witchcraft* (New York: Penguin, 2004), 11.

texts, and firmly articulated theological perspectives, Feri is an ecstatic, experiential tradition that entails each individual practitioner drawing on personal inspiration, direct contact in the spirit realm, and a rich, evolving body of oral lore. Instead of being coven based, the way many Wiccan and Old Craft traditions are, Feri tends to be transmitted directly from a teacher to an individual student, over the course of years. At the end of the training period, there is a singular initiation, as opposed to the hierarchical degree system typical in other witchcraft traditions. It is difficult to parse the precise boundaries of Feri because it is so individualized along these initiatory lines. Like many kinds of witchcraft, it is secretive, and each teacher is charged with passing the tradition according to both their own traditional parameters and also personal revelation.

Another close neighbor of the Feri tradition is Reclaiming, a distinctly feminist, politically engaged tradition of witchcraft founded in the San Francisco Bay Area of California in the late 1970s and early 1980s through the work of Starhawk, Diane Baker, and others. Starhawk would go on to be one of the most influential witches of the twentieth century, and her classic *The Spiral Dance* (1979) remains required reading in many different witch communities, regardless of type. Because both traditions are popular on the West Coast of the United States, and because Starhawk herself was trained in Feri, many Feri initiates are involved in Reclaiming communities, and many Reclaiming witches also privately study and practice Feri. The community focus of Reclaiming complements the transformative, self-exploratory, individualized nature of Feri. Both Reclaiming and Feri witches may or may not understand their traditions as traditional witchcraft, and some practitioners of either may also be comfortable pulling from Wiccan ritual styles and texts. In many ways, Feri is an example of how a single type of witchcraft poses challenges to the categories and distinctions we might try to draw: it is not Wiccan, and yet many individual Feri practitioners today are clearly influenced by Wicca (as was Victor Anderson, by his own account).[24] It is a distinct tradition, and yet it might seem very eclectic and freeform because it pulls from many other systems of magic, including assorted folk traditions, Southern rootwork, Vodou, Huna, and the New Age.

Folk Witchcraft

In recent years, many witches have begun to call their traditions "folk witchcraft" or "folkloric witchcraft." The use of these terms emphasizes the role that folklore and folk tradition play in these types of witchcraft. For some folk witches, this is a way of embracing the contemporary, flexible nature of individual practice. Whereas the term "traditional" sometimes implies historical lineage, organization, and regulation, "folk" points to the personalized, experiential nature of individual practice. It also continues to emphasize the importance of region and culture—who "the folk" are will necessarily change the flavor of the practice! For this reason, folk witches typically identify with additional monikers indicating cultural belonging (e.g., Italian folk witch, Appalachian folk witch, Irish folk witch, etc.). They may also be members of the specific religious groups that are a part of those cultural and regional traditions (e.g., Catholic folk witch, Jewish folk witch, Buddhist folk witch, etc.).

24. Adler, *Drawing Down the Moon*, 79.

Just as we saw within Wicca, there is no universal consensus on exactly where the boundaries of traditional and folk witchcraft are. You are likely to encounter witches who use all of these terms differently, and disagreements abound. It is also worth noting that Wicca and traditional witchcraft are not necessarily mutually exclusive categories, though they may at times appear antagonistic. Within their original British contexts, some Wiccan initiates consider themselves to be practitioners of a traditional witchcraft rooted in England's New Forest. Indeed, in terms of ritual practice and cosmology, these forms of Wicca sometimes resemble their traditional witchcraft cousins more closely than they do the eclectic varieties that prevail in popular publishing and on social media. One of Wicca's most beloved early teachers and liturgists, Doreen Valiente, was also involved in Robert Cochrane's tradition, and her influence shines in both Wiccan and traditional witch spaces.[25] She would ultimately abandon both Gardner and Cochrane in pursuit of her own explorations. In many ways, Valiente is also a model for another theme that we touched on in the last chapter in the context of Wicca, and which warrants a deeper dive as it applies to all kinds of witchcraft: eclecticism.

Blended Traditions

Many of the witches you might encounter today will not identify with Wicca, traditional witchcraft, or any specific branch of folk practice. Though the tendency to create categories and affix labels to ourselves and other people seems to be something of a human

25. Philip Heselton, *Doreen Valiente: Witch* (The Doreen Valiente Foundation in Association with the Centre for Pagan Studies, 2016), 128–37.

impulse, plenty of witches resent being confined to anyone else's box. You are likely to hear plenty of "I'm just a witch!" This makes sense considering how permeable our various witchcraft histories and communities are. There is a great deal of overlap across our traditions, and the increasing prevalence of witchcraft in public spaces creates a lot of room for magical and religious combinations and recombinations. Our vocabularies have shifted as well, meaning that even witches who seem to fit neatly within any particular framework may choose not to use the accompanying jargon to describe themselves. In recent years, it has become popular for some witches, especially in online spaces, to describe their practices with highly specific names rooted in individual proclivities (including aesthetic sensibilities), rather than in something more akin to what we typically think of as "tradition." Thus, a witch with a preference for herbalism or gardening might call themselves a "green witch," and another with a penchant for seaside living and magic involving water might refer to themselves as a "sea witch." There is no limit to this sort of individual labeling, nor is there necessarily any continuity between witches who use the same terms to describe themselves.

Previously, we discussed the development of what came to be called eclectic Wicca, but eclecticism is a broad concept that plays a role in the practices of many non-Wiccan witches as well. Because witchcraft is a movable, permeable category that varies by region, time period, social location, and cultural background, what is included or excluded is highly variable, especially on an individual level. Witchcraft practitioners may include any number of magical systems or techniques, along with any number of religious (or non-religious) frameworks to scaffold them. Sometimes these develop into organized systems and traditions in their own right, but more often the individual witch remains flexible and ever-changing, shifting the nature of their practice as they age, encounter others, learn more, experience difficulty, or as their lives naturally shift. It is common advice in books for would-be practitioners to "keep what works and leave the rest." Witches who identify as eclectic often think of themselves as pragmatists or as explorers. They may experiment widely, developing their practices to precisely tailor their individual interests and needs.

This tendency toward eclecticism is perhaps partially rooted in the need that early proponents of contemporary witchcraft felt to fill in the perceived gaps in their fledgling traditions. Whether they believed they were reconstructing a pagan survival, discovering an underground witch cult, or preserving a secret family tradition, most of the practitioners writing about witchcraft in the twentieth century acknowledged that pieces were missing for one reason or another. These gaps were sometimes filled with ritual forms, magical practices, vocabularies, and fragments of cosmology or philosophy borrowed directly from or inspired by those of other groups. They were also filled with new creations, as witches composed new liturgies inspired by the art, literature, and music of the day. Over the years, some of these compositions have circulated independently of their original sources, with some witches coming to believe that they are older than they really are. More than one claim to antiquity or magical family lineage has been debunked with a little light literary sleuthing! Doreen Valiente, a prolific poet, is probably one of the most frequently (and usually unknowingly) plagiarized. She recounts

tales of seeing her own work published repeatedly with false attribution in her classic book *Witchcraft for Tomorrow* (1978).[26]

Today, eclectic witches are likely to be more selective about their borrowing, as sensitivity surrounding issues of cultural appropriation grows. Not all borrowings are problematic, but concerns for social justice and active efforts to dismantle white supremacy have led to pressing conversations surrounding what have come to be called "open" and "closed" practices—those that can be freely explored, and those that are off-limits to outsiders, respectively. Where these lines are is sometimes a matter of intense debate. If you choose to explore any of these conversations, it is important to begin with and prioritize the perspectives of those within the community in question, rather than those from outside (and especially those outsiders benefiting directly from those borrowings).

Some witches, especially those who see witchcraft as fundamentally a non-religious practice in and of itself, will also actively incorporate their religious backgrounds and interests into their witchcraft. Sometimes, these combinations are surprising or initially seem antithetical to others—for example, when Christians also identify as witches. Witches from a number of religious backgrounds may freely combine their beliefs and practices, and you may encounter practitioners who describe themselves as Christian witches, Jewish witches, Buddhist witches, and more. We saw this earlier in our discussion of folk witchcraft, and such

26. Doreen Valiente, *Witchcraft for Tomorrow* (London: Robert Hale Limited, 2012), 20–21. For examples of Valiente's poetry, *Witchcraft for Tomorrow* also includes a final section called *Liber Umbrarum*, which is a Book of Shadows containing a number of her more well-circulated compositions.

practitioners may or may not identify with the term "eclectic"—the distinction between folk practice and eclectic practice is often a matter of how the individual witch relates to the concept of tradition, as well as their own place within a wider community.

In the spirit of our collective tendency to prefer neat, organized categories, it's not uncommon for this sort of religious blending to inspire derision, both from witches themselves and from members of the religious group in question. However, religious combination is not unique to witches, nor should it imply that these practitioners are somehow ignorant or uncareful. Indeed, the desire to preserve and demarcate a "pure" or "unadulterated" tradition is itself culturally located and contemporary and warrants at least as much interrogation. Many religious movements throughout history have had charismatic members and factions publicly strive to return to a supposedly original, older, or more authentic version of their tradition (this is one of the characteristics of what is sometimes called "fundamentalism"), and this impulse is not unique to any one community, cosmology, region, or political perspective. Blending traditions is not innately problematic (indeed, to some extent it is an inevitability), and the desire to locate a "real" version of any given tradition is not innately benign.[27]

Eclectic forms of witchcraft pull from a variety of sources, including the creativity of the individual witch. Sometimes the end result is a carefully researched and organized practice, consciously developed over time. Other times, the assemblage is unregulated, expansive, and with greater or lesser degrees of

27. Consider that the quest for the "traditional" is sometimes tied to violent nationalist movements.

calculation on the part of the practitioner. Witches who identify with eclecticism may happily call themselves eclectic, but they are equally likely to eschew labels entirely. They may also create their own individualized terms to describe their practices. To some extent, all forms of witchcraft involve what I'm calling eclecticism—borrowing, mixing, religious combination, individual creativity, and fluidity. Where the boundary is between eclecticism and tradition varies (and, depending on whom you ask, may not be real at all).

It would be impossible to assemble a list of "types" or witches that would satisfy and fairly represent an entire movement. Taxonomies are useful ... until they aren't. The world of contemporary witchcraft has expanded to the point where it encompasses such a diverse assortment of beliefs, practices, flavors, aesthetics, and vocabularies that any attempt to neatly codify all of them would fail in short order. Instead, I've considered some of the broader categories that you are sure to encounter, reflecting on where they overlap and how individual practitioners may diverge and blend within these frameworks. Some witches will not fit neatly into one framework, and many will be comfortable in more than one. If the witches you encounter use specific labels for themselves, it is always fair and reasonable to simply ask them, "What do you mean by that?" Most will begin by pointing to (or adamantly away from) one or more of the terms we've discussed: Wiccan, traditional, hereditary, ancestral, folk, or eclectic. None of these terms has a singular meaning, and none is inherently and consistently exclusive of any other.

Suggested Reading

From Scholars

A Republic of Mind and Spirit: A Cultural History of American Metaphysical Religion by Catherine Albanese (New Haven, CT: Yale University Press, 2007)

Useful for thinking about religious combination, blended traditions, and our contemporary conversations surrounding appropriation. You might be surprised by the sorts of borrowings and blendings that Albanese traces.

Enchanted Feminism: The Reclaiming Witches of San Francisco by Jone Salomonsen (London: Routledge, 2002)

Reclaiming is an influential American tradition of witchcraft, and its membership includes some of the most significant writers and teachers in the entirety of contemporary witchcraft. Here is a wonderfully detailed anthropological study of a Reclaiming community in San Francisco.

Wicca: History, Belief, and Community in Modern Pagan Witchcraft by Ethan Doyle White (Brighton, UK: Sussex Academic Press, 2016)

Wicca is one of the most well-documented traditions of contemporary witchcraft, though it continues to be somewhat misunderstood, both by outsiders and by witches themselves. White's survey is accessible and encompassing.

From Witches

Each of these titles is an introduction to a particular type of witchcraft, as described by a practitioner.

American Brujeria: Modern Mexican American Folk Magic by J. Allen Cross (Newburyport, MA: Weiser, 2021)

Traditional Witchcraft: A Cornish Book of Ways by Gemma Gary (Cornwall, UK: Troy Books, 2008)

Folk Witchcraft: A Guide to Lore, Land, and the Familiar Spirit for the Solitary Practitioner by Roger F. Horne (Moon Over the Mountain Press, 2021)

The Crooked Path: An Introduction to Traditional Witchcraft by Kelden (Woodbury, MN: Llewellyn, 2020)

Traditional Wicca: A Seeker's Guide by Thorn Mooney (Woodbury, MN: Llewellyn, 2018)

Betwixt & Between: Exploring the Faery Tradition of Witchcraft by Storm Faerywolf (Woodbury, MN: Llewellyn, 2017)

The Path of the Christian Witch by Adelina St. Clair (Woodbury, MN: Llewellyn, 2010)

Chapter 4

What Witches Do

Even though there are many kinds of contemporary witches, with all manner of beliefs and proclivities, the image of the witch working by candlelight, bent over a brewing cauldron, or chanting in a dark forest prevails in our collective imagination. Witches, whatever else we might think about them, are supposed to have special powers and knowledge that allow them to perform extraordinary feats. If you're like most people, when you think of witchcraft, you probably first think about magic, spells, and rituals. You might associate witches with psychic powers, the ability to talk to the dead, the wisdom to heal or harm with herbal concoctions, and the power to tell the future. Indeed, it is an interest in magic that attracts many people to witchcraft initially. As rich and profound as religious expressions of witchcraft might be, and as useful as it can be for self-development and personal identity, probably the most distinct and enduring characteristic of witchcraft is the practice of magic and ritual. For most of us, a witch just isn't a witch without the power to cast spells and make the seemingly impossible happen!

Some people first come to witchcraft because of prior experiences or seemingly inborn abilities that somehow set them apart from the norm. Many practitioners describe special talents or occurrences that initially made them feel different from others: for example, the experience of prophetic dreams, the tendency to know something will happen before it actually does, or the ability to see or communicate with ghosts or spirits. These practitioners might feel that their identity as a witch is inborn and inherent—only a matter of recognizing what they fundamentally already were. They might begin to engage in more formalized or structured forms of witchcraft (for example, joining a specific tradition, conducting research, or seeking out a coven) in order to control, contain, or hone those abilities. Most witches, however, come to witchcraft because they are interested in developing or awakening these sorts of powers. Witchcraft is not necessarily an inborn state, but rather a tangible skill set that can be learned, practiced, and taught in the way that one might learn a new language or a musical instrument. Newcomers to witchcraft are often attracted by the practices of divination, herbalism, spellcasting, and various kinds of healing, all undertaken for the sake of enriching one's life, improving one's health or fortune, and effecting change in the wider world.

So what are witches actually up to? When someone tells you that they are a witch, what sorts of actions might that entail? In this chapter, we'll take a look at what witches are *doing*. We'll explore some of the most widespread perspectives about magic among witches, as well as the skills and techniques that often go along with a practice of witchcraft. We'll also consider the significant role that healing and self-development frequently play in many kinds of witchcraft, as well as how witches go about

and so may need to begin their work by preparing their space on a more practical level: clearing leaves and other natural debris, picking up litter, or asking permission of local spirits to occupy that space. Some witches see their rituals as deeply religious or spiritual, while others view them as pragmatic, mechanical acts that simply *work* to accomplish specific, secular tasks. In any case, when you hear a witch say, "I'm doing a ritual tonight," or "I'm writing a ritual for my coven," or "Let's do a ritual for that," any of the above may be what they mean, depending on their tradition or their personal style. When they are only doing one step outside of this larger context (for example, casting a spell, performing an offering, doing a tarot reading, praying to a deity), they may not use the term "ritual," as this term tends to imply something more elaborate among witches.

Rituals might be long-standing and passed down from one witch to another, or they may be creative acts, either carefully composed by the individual practitioner for a specific occasion or even improvised on the spot. Some traditions are known for having a body of established rituals that they perform regularly, which fundamentally define the tradition (like Gardnerian or Alexandrian Wicca, both British traditions heavily influenced by fraternal orders like Freemasonry). Others are known for constant change, and characteristically vary widely from group to group (like the Reclaiming tradition of witchcraft, founded in California in the late seventies). Learning to perform, write, and make meaning through the practice of ritual is core for many witches, and new witches often do so by reading rituals in books or sharing rituals online. Most books written for witches contain rituals, and good ritual writers and facilitators are highly valued in witchcraft communities.

Doing Magic

In the last hundred-plus years, an incredible amount of ink has been spilled defining magic, delineating it from religion, and erecting boundaries around who does it, why, and how. Like witchcraft itself, magic is one of those sweeping concepts that potentially includes a lot of different things, and we tend to take for granted that we all mean the same thing just because we're using a shared set of terms. You probably have a general sense of what magic is, but have you ever thought about all the different ways we collectively use that word? When something happens quickly and easily, we might say it was "like magic." When someone asks us for something unreasonable, we might declare, "I'm not a magician!" When someone or something seems fantastical, otherworldly, or just really weird, we might call it "magical." All of these are a little different, but they tell us quite a lot about the prevalent attitudes surrounding magic: it's impossible, it's not of this world, and it might even be crazy! You might also have been taught to believe that magic is childish or ignorant—something only very young or very stupid people believe in—or even that it's evil. In scholarly realms, intellectual giants like Sigmund Freud and Émile Durkheim have famously defined magic as variously a primitive stage of human development and also as fundamentally antisocial and destructive.[28] Magic is what happens when both evolution and the social order fail.

28. Both Freud and Durkheim wrote extensively about magic. For more, consider Sigmund Freud, *Totem and Taboo: Some Points of Agreement between the Mental Lives of Savages and Neurotics*, trans. James Strachey (New York: Norton, 1989), 94–124, and Émile Durkheim, *The Elementary Forms of Religious Life*, trans. Karen E. Fields (New York: The Free Press, 1995), 21–44.

This question of the role of society in determining the boundary around magic turns out to be key, though. Why is it, after all, that some seemingly fantastical things get categorized as magic and others are called religion? Why do we say that a witch lighting a candle to make something happen is doing magic, but someone making a wish over their birthday candles isn't? Why don't we think of priests or pastors as magicians, even when they also purport to be able to perform extraordinary acts? What makes a miracle different from an act of magic?

Often, it turns out, the difference lies in who is doing it. For a number of scholars in the last century, magic necessarily exists outside of the bounds of orderly, accepted society. Actions and beliefs that are widely practiced and regulated might be religion, and they might also be harmless fun (like blowing out birthday candles, no matter how old you are). It's when they belong to outsiders that they become suspect and are likely to be relegated as magic—and therefore crazy, wrong, stupid, or impossible. The ritual cleansing of a person through the application of special water, or the transformation of wine into blood before a room of onlookers isn't dismissed as magic because these particular practices are part of a normalized group of religions—Christianity—and are widely accepted by people in positions of power (though this has certainly not always been the case and isn't the case everywhere in the world). If your neighbor showed you their favorite stick and declared that it gave them power over the land, you might think they were a little nuts or just trying to get a rise out of you, but you probably don't assume the English King Charles is doing the same when he's holding a scepter and being declared ruler because of his special blood. A wand is a wand is a wand, but it's only magic in the hands of the wrong person. As members of a society, we are raised to see some things as perfectly reasonable and expected, and others as bizarre and deviant. Very often, that distinction has little to do with the actual act, but rather who is committing it. Historically, magic is the realm of the marginal: the unregulated, the outsider, the feminine, the poor, the non-European, the non-white, the other. We tend to call things magic when we want to dismiss them.

For contemporary witches, more than practically anything else we could name, the pursuit of magic is essential to life as a witch, and the very act of declaring oneself a witch is out of defiance of the status quo. What exactly magic is and how it works might vary—witches detail a number of definitions, and some of these conflict—but it is, at the very least, a refusal to accept the world as it is handed to us. Many turn to the popular assertion that magic is the power to cause change in accordance with one's will or intention, popularized in the early twentieth century by magicians like Aleister Crowley and Dion Fortune. This perspective often posits that magic is not supernatural or fantastical at all but rather a matter of directing one's mind to influence the outcomes of otherwise natural events. What seems like coincidence is no coincidence at all. It is a series of tiny, interconnected, and perhaps invisible events, any one of which might be altered by the magician to potentially effect great change. Magic, according to this common perspective, operates according to the path of least resistance. To practice it, the magician learns to recognize and take advantage of patterns, creating an environment in which their desires are most probable.

The systems of magic taught by Fortune and Crowley emphasized meditation as a means for controlling the mind and also looked to several Eastern traditions for structure and language concerning the movement of energy naturally occurring in the human body. Magic for many is the process of harnessing this energy for attracting or repelling other forces in the world (also usually described in terms of energy). Energy can then be consciously directed, either toward particular goals or literally into or out of physical objects to alter their character and imbue them with their own powers. For example, a magician might draw special symbols on a blackened mirror and ritually fill it with energy to connect it to other worlds so that it can be used in divination or for communication with spirits. Another example (and one typical of witches) might be directing protective energies into a small object—like a key chain or a piece of jewelry—so that the person carrying it is shielded from harm while traveling.

For many modern magicians, particularly those inspired by the philosophical tradition surrounding Hermeticism—and especially the 1908 Hermetic-inspired New Thought text called *The Kybalion*—one central idea states that thoughts themselves are things, and thinking of something with direction and intention can impact one's reality, both intentionally and not. We can attract good or ill into our own lives through our thoughts. Today, the term "manifestation" is often used to refer to this concept. In recent years manifestation has come to be used interchangeably with magic, though this term sees its origins in systems outside of contemporary witchcraft, especially New Thought and the New Age, which we discussed briefly in chapter 2. The practice of manifestation does not by itself make someone a witch, given its presence in other systems and its relative absence in contemporary witch spaces in earlier decades. In many cases, witches themselves may even eschew the concept, given the ease with which such a perspective can be weaponized to justify suffering, poverty, and other misfortune (if what happens to us is the result of our thoughts, then the blame falls on victims rather than on systemic problems or random chance).

More characteristic of most witchcraft traditions is the perspective that power (a term sometimes used synonymously with energy) innately lies in certain natural objects, like plants and stones, and that a knowledge of this power can be harnessed to aid the witch. One's thoughts and intentions—however focused and directed—are not necessarily enough. Instead, we look to aid from the plants, animals, minerals, and elemental forces that exist in the land around us. These things have properties and qualities that can affect their interactions with humans. Sometimes, those properties are rooted in older systems, like the doctrine of signatures, which purports that a plant's shape, color, or texture indicates its medical usage (for example, a seed pod that resembles human lungs being thought to heal respiratory issues). Sometimes they are the product of folk tradition, generations of experimentation, or lore passed through regional communities or families. Witches draw from these systems and traditions and also experiment to build their own connections and associations. They learn to control their thoughts and draw upon the power of their materials and environments, as well as whatever other abilities they may possess or are developing to perform magic.

Casting Spells

Perhaps more than any other type of magic, spellcasting is the form of magic most consistently associated with witchcraft. We say a witch "put a spell" on someone or something or that they "cast a spell" to make something specific happen. The *Oxford English Dictionary* links the word to much earlier terms related to speaking, writing, and storytelling (we "spell" words and "sit down for a spell" to hear story), and notes that in the seventeenth century it also comes to be tied to the practice of uttering incantations, working charms, or binding someone (especially with our words).[29] For witches today, a spell might be any magical action that is designed to bring about a specific result. Where rituals might be celebratory or religious in nature, spells are usually practical and geared toward creating immediate change in a witch's environment. Very frequently, spells entail the use of material objects (both highly specialized and everyday) combined in a specific way, as well as the magical energy or emotional focus of the witch themselves. The explanation for how a spell works—how it causes something to happen—varies. Some witches believe that it is their thoughts, intentions, and personal energy that effect change, and the materials are not strictly necessary (or can be freely substituted). Others believe that power resides in the spell materials themselves and that the witch must harness and direct it. Most witches subscribe to some combination of these or potentially other models. Some witches also happily embrace the placebo effect! Sometimes just the act of doing the spell can make us feel better, focus us, motivate us, and encourage us to expect positive change, and this should not be dismissed or discounted.

In any case, the casting of spells is a highly symbolic process that depends on the witch having a sophisticated vocabulary of both personal and cultural symbols. We all live in a world of symbols—sports teams have mascots, countries represent themselves with flags, and most of us by now have learned to communicate a

29. *Oxford English Dictionary* (1914), s.v. "spell (v.[4])."

whole range of emotions digitally with emoticons or emoji—this is not unique to witches. In many parts of the world, for example, the color green is associated with money, wealth, prosperity, health, and goodness. Thus, a spell designed to attract money to pay off a debt or to heal a sick person might somehow incorporate the color green (perhaps a witch will burn a green candle with the sick person's name carved into it). Colors have cultural and personal symbolic meaning, but so do plants, animals, shapes, gestures, and sounds. Perhaps you've learned to associate luck with four-leaf clovers or copper coins and lions with strength and authority. Symbols like these are complex and passed cross-culturally, with variations (and sometimes stark differences) across the world. You probably also have deeply individual and personal symbols, unique to you (do you have a song that always makes you think of your mother, or perhaps a lucky number?). Some symbols are considered "traditional" by whatever group uses them, and others may be contemporary, temporary, or highly flexible. The witch consciously harnesses these symbols (and is likely to learn a multitude of symbol systems) for use in spellcasting, creatively combining them to direct their focus and personal energy or power.

Imagine, for example, that a witch wants to cast a spell to perform well on a school-related task. Perhaps they have a test or a presentation coming up that they're nervous about, and they want to make sure they receive a good evaluation. They have an infinite number of symbols to choose from as they start to think about how to craft a spell. If they enjoy astrology, they might choose to perform the spell under particular astrological conditions (perhaps on a Thursday, which is associated with Jupiter, the planet thought to rule over success and prosperity, as well as ideas and education). Burning candles is often relatively easy, so many witches rely on this strategy (in this case, perhaps a yellow one, since yellow is tied to the intellect in some systems of magic, and also more generally to happiness). If they didn't have a candle, perhaps they would rely on what is often called sympathetic magic, in which an object is used to represent or correspond with something else and acting on one is thought to impact the other. In that case, perhaps the witch might take a plain piece of paper, write "Test" or "Exam" at the top, and then award themselves a top grade, physically writing the grade on the paper, along with an imagined note from the teacher praising their work. They may also compose a rhyming couplet to recite or chant repeatedly while doing this, or they may simply state their intention out loud with authority ("I am prepared for my exam and pass with ease!"). They may do all of this while playing a song in the background that motivates them and makes them feel successful or powerful, all while strongly visualizing themselves succeeding.

That's just one simple example! Such a spell could take countless directions. Different witches might accomplish the same thing using very different symbols, different tools, and different words. Much of a witch's time might be spent learning new symbol systems, memorizing correspondences for magic (what herb goes with what planet goes with what body part goes with what ailment?), and crafting and experimenting with spellcasting. Witches perform spells for all manner of practical concerns: prosperity, protection, love, luck, healing, punishing wrongdoing, developing additional powers or skills, and more. For witches, spell crafting and casting are creative acts, and these lie at the heart of witchcraft.

Divination

The practice of divination—the ability to see into the future or obtain knowledge that would otherwise not be available—is central in all kinds of witchcraft, in one form or another. For many witches, divination is a substantial part of their practice. They learn to read tarot cards, use a pendulum, read tea leaves, dowse, interpret runes, communicate with ancestors or other spirits, and even concoct their own individual systems. Many witches will perform divination before undertaking other magical acts, checking first that a spell or ritual is necessary or will be successful. They may modify their specific plans based on the result of this divination—or forgo the magical working entirely if their divining reveals potential problems. For other witches, the act of divination itself is core to their entire practice. They may work as tarot readers or other types of fortune tellers, providing services to clients or within their immediate communities. The term "readers" has been widely adopted to refer to many types of diviners, beyond those that use tarot, so the phrases "do a reading" or "get a reading" may mean that various tools and techniques are involved. Some witches make a living doing this, either providing readings or teaching others how to perform readings. Other witches use divination privately, as an aid to their own magical work or personal development.

Healing

For many practitioners, the function of the witch is primarily that of a healer. In the same way that legend and lore tell of the witch as a figure with the capacity to heal illness, aid with pregnancy and birth, and traverse the spirit realm to bring back valuable knowledge for others, the contemporary witch is often much the same. Aside from working spells that center healing, many witches learn holistic, traditional, or "alternative" healing practices, which include herbalism, hypnosis, crystal healing, energy healing, and assorted other methodologies. Some witches feel so strongly about this that they feel called to practice within allopathic medicine, training as conventional doctors, nurses, paramedics, and EMTs. They may also become midwives or doulas, as well as therapists and counselors. Mental health is a central concern for many witches, and newcomers to witchcraft are sometimes attracted to the prospect of self-healing, self-care, and the therapeutic. Many practitioners frame their witchcraft within the bounds of psychology—a creative way to alter their thought patterns to be more productive and healthier, to address and recover from past traumas, or to develop a stronger sense of self and personal value. Witchcraft is often described by these practitioners as a means for real-world personal development, helping them better assert themselves, break negative habits or generational patterns, create personal meaning, or otherwise grow into better versions of themselves.

In a similar vein, witches may also be inclined to see themselves as public servants, serving the emotional, practical, and magical needs of their communities by offering an assortment of services. These might include the aforementioned counseling (both conventional and spiritual), as well as mentoring, volunteering, working in education, working in the court system (social work is not an uncommon field for witches to occupy), or running community pantries and gardens. For many witches, the image of the witch as a healer—and often a misunderstood healer or a healer for the marginalized—is central and becomes a sacred or magical calling. Some traditions of witchcraft require members to train formally in one or more healing modalities, while others assume that the committed witch will eventually acquire them as their practice grows and develops.

Sacred Time

For many witches of all types and traditions, one of the most important goals of their practice is to build connections with the natural world and its various cycles. This is for the purpose of living a more balanced and meaningful life and also working more effective magic. Witchcraft tends to emphasize embodied experience and the material realm, as well as power and a sense of the sacred located in nature, and so many of the most popular and common types of rituals focus on emotionally, spiritually, or physically tuning in to the witch's environment. This might mean celebrating holidays tied to the changing seasons, tracking the phases of the moon or the movement of other celestial bodies, or marking various life stages with rites of passage. Witches with practices closely tied to the land they live on may conduct ritual around the blooming of particular trees or the arrival of certain migratory animals. Many witches learn to garden, forage, or hunt as a part of their efforts to learn and work with natural cycles, believing that materials gathered in this way are more powerful and beneficial than those that are acquired out of season, imported, or produced by someone else. Witches may also focus on bodily cycles, ritually marking things like menstruation or aging. In all these cases, we see a sense of the sacred—whether explicitly in a religious sense or not—attached to the passage of time and the resulting observable changes in the world.

One of the most prevalent examples of how contemporary witches connect magically or spiritually to natural cycles is through the performance of rituals according to the phases of the moon. Most witches believe that the moon exerts magical influence in their lives and consciously incorporate its movements into their practice. A waxing moon, for example, is usually thought to be an auspicious time to cast spells that entail increase, completion, or otherwise drawing desirable things toward oneself (like wealth, a new romantic relationship, or a promotion at work). A waning moon, in contrast, is an ideal time to decrease or push something away (like an illness, a string of bad luck, or a toxic relationship). Both full moons and new moons are also ascribed particular significance. Many covens choose to meet on full moons, and witches may choose to leave their various magical tools outside or in a window to absorb the moon's light, charging them for use in ritual later. New moons are often reserved for reflection and various kinds of introspective personal work, sometimes tied to death and the underworld, or used for other matters related to darkness, mystery, or the invisible. Some witches also abstain from performing magic at this time. Each phase of the moon holds significance, along with special events like eclipses, blue moons, or super moons. In some traditions of witchcraft, the moon is tied mythologically to specific deities or spirits, and witches who are invested in these are likely to ascribe additional significance to the moon beyond its magical influence.

Witches are also likely to have an interest in astrology. In the same way that the moon is thought to influence magical workings, the body, and even a person's moods, so too do the movements of planets and stars. Witches often tie planets and constellations to specific personal and social concerns: for example, connecting Venus to matters of love and Mars to matters of conflict. They may consult horoscopes and make choices based on astrological timing or the zodiac signs of the people involved.

The celebration of seasonal cycles may include a wide variety of established festivals and holidays originating in times and regions all over the world, according to the individual practitioner's cultural or religious background. The latter half of the twentieth century also saw the development of a particular seasonal calendar rooted in the British agricultural cycle, along with influences from Celtic and Germanic traditions, and codified as what many now call the Wheel of the Year. The Wheel of the Year was initially conceived in the works of Gerald Gardner and originally consisted of four high holy days, called sabbats: May Eve, August Eve, November Eve, and February Eve.[30] The summer and winter solstices and the fall and spring equinoxes were subsequently (and quickly) added by Gardnerian witches, and the eight-spoked Wheel of the Year was born. The sabbats were shortly adopted by one of Gardner's contemporaries, Ross Nichols, the founder of a popular modern Druid movement called the Order of Bards, Ovates & Druids.[31] Their popularity grew rapidly, with various witch and Pagan groups adopting this set of festivals, sometimes changing their names to reflect their respective regions. The Wheel of the Year is now ubiquitous in contemporary Pagan, witch, and metaphysical spaces. Many of the traditions, names, and associations with these holidays are

30. Gerald Gardner, *Witchcraft Today*, 50th anniv. ed. (New York: Citadel Press, 2004), 130.

31. Ronald Hutton, *The Triumph of the Moon: A History of Modern Pagan Witchcraft*, 2nd ed. (New York: Oxford University Press, 2019), 256.

rooted in much older cultural traditions and regional folk practice, but their current articulation is directly the result of the influence of Wicca and the work of Gerald Gardner.

Today, the Wheel of the Year is celebrated by many kinds of witches, both Wiccan and non-Wiccan, and includes Halloween (sometimes called Samhain), the winter solstice (popularly called Yule), Imbolc (also called Candlemas or Feast of Torches), the spring equinox (sometimes called Ostara), Beltane (also called May Day or May Eve), the summer solstice (sometimes called Litha or Midsummer), Lammas (also called August Eve or Lughnasadh), and the fall equinox (sometimes called Mabon). Like festivals in other traditions, both religious and secular, the eight sabbats can variously entail gift-giving, parties, games, feasts, and special rituals. These eight sabbats have become so popular that in the United States they are included in the academic calendars of some colleges and universities and are also eligible for religious absences at some workplaces. In some parts of Europe, where these festivals originate, they are still celebrated in ways that reflect national or regional tradition, passed on as they always have been through local folkways. These types of celebrations may bear little resemblance to how contemporary Pagans and witches celebrate them, especially as they have transformed through their transmission to other countries and regions, especially North America. The Wheel of the Year is an example of something that is both very modern and also deeply rooted in the past, which is a theme we see over and over again in contemporary witchcraft as a whole.

In recent years, many witches have moved away from the Wheel of the Year as described in Wicca and those Pagan traditions inspired by Wicca. Some feel that these European-based traditions make little sense outside of their original contexts and have modified them to reflect their own regions. Because the ultimate goal for many witches is to connect with the natural landscape, they instead choose to create their own traditions based on the local environment. Other witches practice traditions that celebrate other holidays entirely. Popular days include Walpurgisnacht and Lupercalia, but you are likely to encounter many others if you have much interaction with different kinds of witches.

Rituals that mark the passage of time are one way that practitioners build connection, to the earth, to the past, and to their communities. It is common advice for new witches to begin by either observing the phases of the moon or celebrating the Wheel of the Year (and possibly designing their own Wheel of the Year). Some of these traditions and practices are recent and reflect contemporary trends and interests, while others are rooted in history. Public events like open rituals and Pagan festivals are often held in conjunction with sabbats, full moons, or other special days, and these celebrations are good opportunities for mingling with witches in more casual settings, as well as typical entry points to practice for aspiring witches.

One of the reasons why witchcraft as a whole can be difficult to understand, especially within the confines of only a religious framework, is because it often does not prioritize a *belief* system. For most witches, witchcraft is first and foremost an action—a thing that you *do*. The practice of witchcraft includes spellcasting, divination, healing, and various kinds of ritual. Not surprisingly, you are sure to encounter disagreement about how to practice, how often, and what the difference is between a witch, someone who is practicing another sort of magic, and someone who is merely dabbling. Because these conversations are so central and contentious, and because witchcraft collectively emphasizes practice over belief, we have begun by focusing on action. However, belief and practice are not discrete categories—one implies the other—and many witches *do* understand their witchcraft as rooted fundamentally in particular belief systems. In the next chapter, we'll take a look at some of those beliefs!

Suggested Reading

From Scholars

Magic: A History by Chris Gosden (New York: Picador, 2020)

A sweeping world survey of magic and its role in human civilization, written for a general audience. This book is useful for thinking about how witchcraft fits into a much wider history.

Lived Religion: Faith and Practice in Everyday Life by Meredith B. McGuire (Oxford: Oxford University Press, 2008)

Most of us are used to thinking about religion and spiritual practice as defined by formal institutions, which often obscures how it looks on the ground among everyday people. This book is useful for thinking about how religion (and by extension magic and ritual) actually looks and functions in day-to-day life.

Stations of the Sun: A History of the Ritual Year in Britain by Ronald Hutton (Oxford: Oxford University Press, 1996)

Many of the most popular witchcraft holidays and festivals are rooted in British tradition. This is a detailed, highly engaging history that will be of service to readers well beyond a study of witchcraft.

Making Magic: Religion, Magic, and Science in the Modern World by Randall Styers (Oxford: Oxford University Press, 2004)

What's the relationship between religion, science, and magic, and how have the three worked to define each other today? Styers provides us with tools for thinking about why magic persists and how it has helped to shape modernity.

From Witches

Each of these focuses on the practice of magic and various types of ritual, from the perspective of different sorts of witches. All of the below contain spells, rituals, and exercises designed to help readers discover and develop their own power.

Year of the Witch: Connecting with Nature's Seasons through Intuitive Magick by Temperance Alden (Newburyport, MA: Weiser, 2020)

Psychic Witch: A Metaphysical Guide to Meditation, Magick & Manifestation by Mat Auryn (Woodbury, MN: Llewellyn, 2020)

Wild Witchcraft: Folk Herbalism, Garden Magic, and Foraging for Spells, Rituals, and Remedies by Rebecca Beyer (New York: Simon Element, 2022)

New World Witchery: A Trove of North American Folk Magic by Cory Thomas Hutcheson (Woodbury, MN: Llewellyn, 2021)

The Element Encyclopedia of 5000 Spells by Judika Illes (London: HarperElement, 2004)

Spell Bound: A New Witch's Guide to Crafting the Future by Chaweon Koo (Melbourne, Australia: Smith Street Books, 2022)

Life Ritualized: A Witch's Guide to Honoring Life's Important Moments by Phoenix LeFae and Gwion Raven (Woodbury, MN: Llewellyn, 2021)

Blood Sex Magic: Everyday Magic for the Modern Mystic by Bri Luna (New York: HarperCollins, 2023)

Chapter 5

What Witches Believe

Whether or not an individual witch thinks of their craft as religious, spiritual, secular, or something else entirely, their worldview is one rooted in enchantment. For witches, life is filled with potential beyond that which is readily seen. It may come through in the form of elaborate rituals, the practice of spellcasting, or just the assurance of an additional layer of wonder undergirding the mundane world. On the surface their life might look very typical—they go to work, raise their children, pay bills, and get frustrated in traffic—but that life is informed and augmented by a relationship with the magical. This might include deciphering signs and symbols in everyday occurrences using divination to make decisions, or it could include making offerings to ancestors or deities at a home altar to incur protection or cultivate wisdom. Witches believe that they can take magical action to impact the world around them, and the primary way that they do this is by building and maintaining special relationships beyond what we might think of as typical, everyday reality. For many witches, those relationships are quite literal: they meet, speak to, work with, worship, and otherwise interact with deities, ancestors, land spirits, the dead, and other entities. For other witches, those relationships are with the natural world, their communities, or with their own personal power and sense of self.

In this chapter, we'll take a look at the various "-isms" in witchcraft. What do witches believe? How do those beliefs and perspectives impact how witches move through the world? You may already be familiar with polytheism, animism, or pantheism, but witches occupy an enchanted world that includes all of these and more. As we've seen, witchcraft doesn't tend to emphasize belief the way we are accustomed to when thinking about the breadth of what we might call religion or spirituality. For most witches, their craft is about practice—*doing* rather than believing. However, belief and practice aren't inherently distinct things. One informs the other, and even witches who assert that their practices are purely operative or secular still hold beliefs about the world that shine through in the actions they take.

A World Full of Spirits and Energy

The witch's world is alive with all manner of spirits, both metaphorical and very real. Some of those spirits are sure to be familiar to you, even if only from the pages of fantasy novels or folktales: deities, angels, saints, demons, fairies, the dead, familiars, and any number of plant, animal, or mineral spirits. Sometimes, the primary spirit that a witch works with is their own—the unique soul or higher self, embodied in their own being. Sometimes, in an extension of our own human creativity, we come to see our emotions, proclivities, passions, and challenges as spirits too. In making such abstractions a little more concrete, it becomes easier to manage and direct them, allowing witches to live more balanced, fruitful, and joyful lives.

Witches interact with spirits in many ways, from lengthy rehearsed ritual to spontaneous prayer to casual conversations that take place as the witch goes about their day. Even when the spirit in question is of a variety that overlaps with other traditions or religions—for example, a Catholic saint, a demon described in a medieval European magical book called a grimoire, or a fairy prone to appearing in classic children's stories—it is likely that the individual witch has a unique understanding of that figure that won't necessarily align with every other interpretation you may have seen before. Witches often look to literature, history, art, and popular culture for inspiration or precedent, and because so many believe that these various entities are present and relevant today, it stands to reason that they continue to interact with humans, and they can grow and change over time. This means that the stories we might tell about them never really end. Deities might continue to reveal knowledge, fairies may develop a taste for the modern, and saints may redefine their interests and agendas in accordance with societal change. Even a historically terrifying and much-maligned figure like Satan becomes a symbol of self-reliance, independent thinking, or dissent in the face of oppression for the witches who choose to work with him. This is because, regardless of tradition, one of the very basic premises of witchcraft is that we can experience our own world directly, taking control of our impact within it and enjoying an active role in how it is shaped. This means that the spiritual entities we work with and believe in interact with us directly, and they grow and change as our own human world does.

Witches also believe that the objects they use in magic—ritual tools, herbs, crystals, and more—have qualities beyond what most people would suppose, whether inherently or because the witch has willed it to be so. In our previous discussion of magic, we touched on the subject of energy, which is a general term for a metaphysical force that exists both in living things and in objects. Magic often entails moving energy in and out of objects. Sometimes witches speak of this energy as neutral and universal, ebbing and flowing and able to be manipulated by anyone with the knowledge and skill to do so. One does not need to *believe* in energy from the witch's perspective. It is a neutral, almost mechanical force that exists in the world and operates according to particular parameters, like electricity. Other times, witches speak of energy as possessing a kind of consciousness, going where it's needed, or permanently residing in particular places, people, or things, impacting their character over time. This belief in energy lends the everyday an otherworldly nature, such that even if a witch doesn't believe in other sorts of entities, their cosmology is still a deeply enchanted one.

Relationships with Gods

For many witches, the central focus of their witchcraft is a specific deity or group of deities. These deities may be familiar to you from childhood explorations of Greek, Celtic, or Norse mythology, or they may be very contemporary, popularized through modern sources or even rooted in fiction or pop culture. They might be deities with extensive histories and source material from the ancient world, or they may be obscure, with much of their mythos partially reconstructed, gaps filled in with an individual witch's personal experience and creative suppositions.[32] Some witches may operate within established religious frameworks, like Christianity or Judaism, and maintain relationships with deities or other spiritual entities (like saints or the Virgin Mary) associated with those cosmologies. Other witches see the various deities described across time throughout the world as aspects or disparate forces of a universal, all-encompassing divine force, sometimes interpreted as an unspecified "Spirit," the "All," or sometimes the "Divine Mind." Some witchcraft traditions, especially organized initiatory traditions, center upon the worship of specific deities who may be unique to those traditions. Others leave the choice to individuals as a matter of personal preference. Many witches have relationships with several different deities, even from different pantheons. It's not uncommon for witches to be drawn to different deities at different stages of their practice and over the course of their lives.

The roles of gods in witchcraft can be confusing precisely because of the enormous variety that exists. An individual witch might feel comfortable with particular familiar descriptions for their theological views—like polytheism, animism, or pantheism—but those views may be vastly different from their fellow witches. Further complicating matters is that even those witches who do incorporate deities into their craft—and many witches don't, as we shall see—are likely to talk about and relate to them somewhat differently from the monotheistic religions that most of us are accustomed to treating as normative. Thanks to the

32. Witches sometimes refer to these individualized conclusions—reached through magical experimentation, intuition, or direct encounters with deities themselves—as "unverifiable personal gnosis" (UPG for short). UPG, as you can probably imagine, is a hot topic for debate among practitioners, especially where the UPG of different witches conflicts.

influence of Christianity in particular, we tend to collectively think of gods as omniscient, omnipotent, parent-like, or inaccessible without intermediaries like priests or ministers. For most theistic witches, however, deities are usually much more immediate and even humanlike.

Witches are prone to describing gods as possessing preferences, like favorite foods or animals, as well as unique prerequisites for interacting with humans. They are also likely to rule over specific realms (like the underworld or heaven), types of people (like mothers or soldiers), trades or crafts (like weaving, blacksmithing, or even witchcraft itself), or places (like forests, markets, or battlefields). Rarely in witchcraft are gods portrayed as all-knowing or all-powerful. Indeed, often they are not even particularly invested in humans at all. Witches as a whole—regardless of their particular persuasions—abhor proselytizing, and this is reflected in how they relate to their gods. Usually it is the individual who must approach the deity, as the accrual of followers is not thought to be a central desire. Even where a witch does feel that the relationship was initiated by the deity, there is often still an emphasis on personal choice to maintain it. Many witches will engage in the practice of specific rituals or the making of devotional offerings in order to first establish that connection.

Also distinct in witchcraft spaces is the tendency to speak of deities in terms of partnerships or working relationships instead of relying on the language of worship. Because the emphasis is normally on personal choice, consent, and reciprocity, witches are considerably more likely to declare that they "work with" a particular god rather than that they "worship" or "serve" them. A working relationship might entail the witch providing ritual offerings in exchange for knowledge—for example, if a deity rules over a particular skill the witch seeks to acquire. Often, witches will approach deities in search of self-development, healing, wisdom, protection, or power. Offerings may include perishables like food or drink, consumed in ritual or placed on an altar for a designated period of time (and then ritually disposed of). They may also include non-material gifts like poetry, music, or even research conducted in the deity's honor. Some witches may make offerings through the body: for example, by wearing head coverings, adopting a special diet, or acquiring devotional tattoos or piercings.

Even when witches do prefer to speak of worship and service, this should not imply that they are sacrificing their power or autonomy. Witches of all kinds still value self-authority, and this generally precludes entering into relationships of any kind that compromise their own free will. That includes divine relationships! The most devout witch priest is sure to have some expectation of reciprocity, even if it is only the desire for connection and orientation in a wider world.

Though outwardly it might appear that most witches are polytheists, the spectrum of beliefs included by this relatively vague term is vast. Some witches, for example, do not see the gods as literal beings with their own agency but rather as mythological constructions representing human abstractions, like love or justice or compassion. The act of engaging with them as metaphors is no less real or powerful for such witches, who may identify as archetypists or atheists as readily as polytheists. Belief—especially literal belief—is not always particularly important. Instead, the emphasis lies on ritual action. For these witches, it might be acceptable to interchange similar deities, creating conflations based on shared characteristics. Sometimes conflation and interchange occur because the witch believes these "smaller" deities to be a reflection of a larger, less personable entity, whether a supreme God or Goddess or an abstract divine "source." This perspective is sometimes called "soft polytheism," as opposed to "hard polytheism."

Another popular variation on the divine is present in what is sometimes called the "Goddess movement." Though many of its roots lie in the mid-twentieth-century works of poet Robert Graves (especially his 1948 classic *The White Goddess*), the Goddess—often depicted as a representation of the sacred feminine itself, with or without any particular name—really came to the fore uniquely in the feminist witchcraft popularized in the 1970s and 1980s by authors like Starhawk, Merlin Stone, and Monica Sjöö, especially in the United States. Witches who are deeply invested in the overthrowal of patriarchy, the reclamation of women's authority and autonomy, and the healing of an embattled planet (often understood to be a physical embodiment of the Goddess, possessing feminine pronouns and qualities) are often drawn to this expression of the divine. The Goddess is often portrayed as a triad—maiden, mother, and crone—representing the supposed stages of a woman's lifespan.

Though today many witches do not explicitly identify as Goddess worshippers, the influence of this movement on witchcraft as a whole has been substantial. The maiden-mother-crone model shows up attached to deities that were not historically structured as such, along with the assumption that witchcraft is inherently tied to women's liberation. These witches are also likely to see themselves as spiritual descendants of the European witch hunts, which they might construe (with greater and lesser degrees of historical accuracy) as fundamentally being about women's oppression. Recent conversations around gender and inclusivity have led to many witches today distancing themselves from the Goddess movement, which in its efforts to create space for women has also seen the capacity for both gender essentialism and transphobia. Other Goddess worshippers are actively working to expand and develop the movement to include a wider spectrum of practitioners, deeply investing their witchcraft in social justice.

In conjunction with all these models (and potentially many more), witches describe their divine relationships on a kind of spectrum. Some take oaths to specific deities or join special orders, becoming part of a priesthood and seeking out community roles comparable to those filled by clergy in other religious groups. You are also likely to hear the terms "dedicant" or "devotee," which also indicate some kind of long-term commitment. Witches may also have more casual relationships with certain gods, working with them only for specific purposes or at certain times of their lives. Just like human relationships, not all divine partnerships are permanent or even particularly deep. And just like human relationships, either party may be responsible for beginning or ending them. Sometimes a witch feels called to work with a specific deity. They may feel it so strongly that it doesn't seem voluntary (and for some, it may not be). Most witches, however, choose to research and explore gods that appeal to them for whatever reason, building a practice over time with the aid of guidance from more experienced witches, books or online media, or their personal experiments and intuition.

Ancestors and the Dead

Witchcraft has long been associated with the dead, and for good reason. Witches believe that the world includes more than we can readily see—our bodies and the physical realm aren't the full picture. It makes sense, then, that most of us don't see death of the body as the end. There is no single belief among witches about what happens after death. Many witches believe in reincarnation. Wicca, for example, tends to see the world as a series of repeating cycles. In the same way that the seasons change over the course of the year, our lives begin and end and then begin again. Time is cyclical rather than linear, and so there really is no such thing as a true ending. Some believe that the purpose of reincarnation is to return over and over again to develop, learning spiritual lessons and ultimately reuniting with the divine. This idea was heavily popularized by the teachings of the Theosophical Society, that influential esoteric movement founded in New York in 1875 that we met briefly in chapter 2. Meanwhile, Spiritualists taught that souls reside in a land of rest and recuperation called Summerland and were not necessarily reincarnated.[33] Variations on this belief in Summerland (or sometimes the plural "the Summerlands") persists among some witches, even though both Theosophy's and Spiritualism's popularity has subsided among witches today. The influence of both movements is readily apparent among many kinds of contemporary witchcraft, as well as in other spiritual and religious communities.

33. For an exploration of these influential movements and their impact on many popular beliefs about reincarnation, consider *Recycled Lives: A History of Reincarnation in Blavatsky's Theosophy* by Julie Chajes (New York: Oxford University Press, 2019).

Some witches believe that upon death we dwell among our ancestors in a world parallel to our own. Ancestral spirits are thought to watch over their descendants, maintaining a keen interest in the affairs of the living and providing aid upon request. They may even still take pleasure in the material and enjoy receiving offerings of favorite food and drink from when they were still living. Ancestral spirits are usually thought to have access to additional power and knowledge, and so witches may consult them for assistance in times of trouble. It is common for witches to maintain ancestor shrines or altars in their homes containing mementos, photographs, candles, and whatever offerings the witch deems appropriate. Often, ancestors are familial, but sometimes particular traditions have their own ancestral pantheons, tied together by a magical or spiritual lineage rather than a genetic one. Some witches may also include people who were just very impactful, like favorite artists, political leaders, or other historical figures they feel a connection with. When newcomers to witchcraft seek advice on where to begin, they are likely to be told to start with their own ancestors. This leads many witches to become interested in genealogy. Witches interact with ancestors through offerings, through ritual, through divination, and through the interpretation of signs in everyday life.

Because witches usually believe that death is not the end of consciousness, they are also inclined to the paranormal. This includes belief in ghosts and hauntings. Aside from ancestor veneration, witches may also communicate with the dead for other purposes. Some witches develop this as a specialty, offering services like clearing hauntings or assisting the dead to cross over into an afterlife. Some witches identify as necromancers, making communication with the dead a cornerstone of their entire practice.

There are no universally held witch beliefs about afterlives or the nature of death, except perhaps that the dead are significant, even if only as symbols of connection or a source of inspiration or comfort. Many witches never take an interest in deities or other kinds of spirits, focusing entirely on ancestor veneration and other work with the dead. For these witches, their relationship with the dead is core to their identity. For some, this is *the* thing that defines a witch, and witches who don't engage in these practices are using the term incorrectly.

Sacred Nature

Have you ever had the experience of looking into the night sky and being so overcome by its vastness that you felt genuine awe for the power and beauty of the universe? Maybe thinking about the depths of the ocean makes you wonder at the profound creativity of life. Perhaps it is the deep woods that intrigue you, or the seemingly impossible migrations of whales or butterflies. The wilderness has been unnerving people for millennia, inspiring us alternately to venture out with full packs and an adventurous spirit or to demonize it with tales of devils, savage cryptids bent on devouring human flesh, or ghostly spirits who lure travelers in to never return. We love nature and we abhor it, all at the same time. We work tirelessly to keep it out of our homes, while glorifying it as a mystical place of self-discovery, self-reliance, and intrepidness.

In many ways, witchcraft can be a way of grappling with all these tensions. Much of the scholarship available on contemporary witchcraft traditions—especially that which focuses on European traditions, contemporary Paganism, and witchcraft in the United States—refers to witches collectively as participating in "nature religion" or sometimes "nature-based religion." This is because so many types of witchcraft have been rooted in observing various kinds of natural cycles, like the changing seasons or the phases of the moon. It is also because of the prevalence of both pantheism and animism in many kinds of witchcraft, both of which may lead witches to believe that the divine or various kinds of spiritual entities reside in the physical world. Environmentalist and feminist movements have also intersected, especially in the latter quarter of the twentieth century in the United States, when it was particularly popular to speak of "Mother Nature" with ubiquity. The assault on the planet came to be tied with not just human negligence, but patriarchy, and parallel to the oppression of women.

Of course, the personification of nature—and the feminization of nature—is nothing new in human history, but for some witches the divinity of the planet Earth is quite literal. Many witches see the earth as the physical embodiment of a Mother Goddess. Their witchcraft is focused on both building a sacred connection to the earth, and also healing the relationship between the planet and human beings, who are responsible for so much environmental destruction. This is especially true in many kinds of Wiccan witchcraft, which often sees the Wiccan Goddess and God as embodiments of the forces of nature. The celebration of the Wheel of the Year—the eight seasonal holidays derived from an assortment of historical and contemporary sources—serves as a means of connecting with the land and its natural cycles. Many other kinds of witches also celebrate the Wheel of the Year or some other assortment of magically significant days rooted in the change of the seasons. On top of seasonal holidays, witches often express a sense of the sacred tied to nature through the desire to ritually attune to the phases of the moon or the movement of other celestial bodies.

Another way that witches emphasize nature as a source of magic and the sacred is through their own bodies. In most kinds of contemporary witchcraft, the body is viewed as natural, powerful, honorable, and even holy. The body is a source of magical energy, which can be harnessed and channeled through outwardly mundane things like dancing, working out, or sex. Witches are likely to be more accepting and open when it comes to matters of sexuality and physical indulgence, because taking pleasure in the body is considered natural and healthy. Witches are as susceptible to societal messages about desirable bodies and the more toxic elements of wellness culture as any other group, but by and large you should expect to see more acceptance for difference kinds of bodies, as well as all of the ways that humans have found to enjoy them. Many witches take self-care and physical and emotional wellness to be an expression of their magical or spiritual practice, and so many become involved in both conventional and alternative healing modalities. The sacredness of the human body is central to many kinds of witchcraft, and many people who explore witchcraft come because they are seeking some form of healing or a sense of sacred connection to themselves.

Though the phrases "earth-based religion" and "nature-based religion" are common and often used sweepingly (especially by scholars and journalists), they can also be a little misleading. First, as we have seen repeatedly, not all witches see their practice of witchcraft as religious. One need not sacralize nature in order to value it or even to make it central to a practice of magic. Witches with heavily land-based practices may work to learn about local wildlife and native plant life in order to serve as caretakers. Many witches believe that incorporating a local element into magic makes it more effective and personal, for example using native plants or minerals instead of importing herbs or crystals from other parts of the world. Witches are also likely to challenge the anthropocentric notion that "nature" is something set apart from the human world and that we are somehow exempt from its cycles and laws because of our long-supposed specialness. Human beings are animals, like any other, equally dependent on the land and subject to its fate. Our cities, our homes, and our physical bodies are all equally a part of nature, because there is no escaping nature. None of these perspectives necessarily requires a religious framework to be meaningful or important to the witch who holds them. Second, the reliance on calling witchcraft "nature-based" obscures the many traditions that are not! Not all witches celebrate seasonal cycles, enjoy practicing outdoors, or are heavily invested in environmentalism. For many witches, their practices are simply focused elsewhere (like on a particular deity who isn't tied to nature or on the working of practical magic for myriad other purposes), and this doesn't make them any less witches.

In keeping with a common theme, how witches think about spirits, deities, ancestors, and nature can vary dramatically. Some witches are atheists, while others are devoted priests. Some witches believe in and work with demons, angels, fairies, and any number of other entities. Many witches practice some sort of ancestor veneration and work with the spirits of the dead, whether that's in the realm of the paranormal or as necromancers. Whether they are religious, spiritual, secular, or prefer another term entirely, it is fair to say that witches live in a world that is more than what many other people suppose. The world of witchcraft is an enchanted one, though the nature of that enchantment exists on a spectrum.

Suggested Reading

From Scholars

Sex, Death and Witchcraft: A Contemporary Pagan Festival by Douglas Ezzy (London: Bloomsbury Academic, 2014)

An analysis of the spiritual perspectives present at a single Australian festival and representative of wider communities, with a focus on the notion of "lived religion" rather than belief alone.

The Golden Bough by James Frazer, 1 vol. abridged ed. (New York: Touchstone, 1996)

The work of James Frazer is not explicitly about witchcraft, but his influence on witchcraft and occult communities cannot be overstated. Frazer's comparative analysis of deities (however dubious by today's scholarly standards) persists among witches, even though many today are not directly familiar with his work.

Pan: The Great God's Modern Return by Paul Robichaud (London: Reaktion Books, 2021)

A fascinating example of how a deity might develop and take on different meanings with the movements (literary and religious) that adopt them.

Cunning Folk and Familiar Spirits: Shamanistic Visionary Traditions in Early Modern British Witchcraft and Magic by Emma Wilby (Brighton, UK: Sussex Academic Press, 2005)

Wilby's research is in early modern practice and not the contemporary, but her publications have done much to inspire witches today.

From Witches

Each of these illustrates a specific model for enchanted relationships, whether with deities, ancestors, nature, or spirits.

Queen of All Witcheries: A Biography of the Goddess by Jack Chanek (Woodbury, MN: Llewellyn, 2023)

Fairycraft: Following the Path of Fairy Witchcraft by Morgan Daimler (Winchester, UK: Moon Books, 2016)

Magickal Mediumship: Partnering with Ancestors for Healing and Spiritual Development by Danielle Dionne (Woodbury, MN: Llewellyn, 2020)

What Is Remembered Lives: Developing Relationships with Deities, Ancestors & the Fae by Phoenix LeFae (Woodbury, MN: Llewellyn, 2019)

The Horned God of the Witches by Jason Mankey (Woodbury, MN: Llewellyn, 2021)

Anatomy of a Witch: A Map to the Magical Body by Laura Tempest Zakroff (Woodbury, MN: Llewellyn, 2021)

Chapter 6

The Witch's Materials

Walk into any witchcraft or metaphysical supply store and you will instantly be struck by how much *stuff* seems to be involved in being a witch. Thousands of items grace the pages of online retailers too, from books to dried herbs, from crystals to robes, from cauldrons to animal bones, and well beyond. Scrolling through social media hashtags quickly reveals the special emphasis placed not only on these precious objects but also on material beauty as a whole. Artfully filtered images of elaborate altars garner thousands of likes and shares, and witch influencers offer advice on coordinating outfits that correspond to magical intentions or makeup looks designed to augment the energy of specific moon phases or personal astrological placements. Every corner of the internet seems to include advertisements for various products and services—magical day planners, candles designated for various ritual purposes, bespoke tarot decks, all manner of jewelry featuring occult symbols—immediately at the fingertips of the magically inclined, whether they think of themselves as witches or merely as enthusiasts. Some of this deep investment in the material and the aesthetic is perhaps a reflection of the role that capitalism, social media, and the pressures of the marketplace seem to broadly have on most every religious group or niche community we might observe (a cynic might remark that there's potentially a market for everything!), but it is also because witchcraft as a whole tends to locate both power and the sacred in the material world.

One of the central features of witchcraft of all kinds is the power it grants practitioners to imbue all kinds of objects with both magical and spiritual significance. Part of becoming a witch and developing a personal witchcraft practice entails deciding what material channels one prefers for working magic. That means selecting from traditional tools but also relocating witchcraft into one's creative projects and the everyday. Witchcraft is as much an art as it is a religion or a practice, and this is part of the appeal for many. Witches learn to work with a number of magical objects you've likely heard about or seen in movies—ceremonial daggers, crystal balls, magic wands, and more—as well as creating their own personal tools, unique to their individual proclivities and interests (and perhaps not immediately identifiable to onlookers as witchcraft at all). In this chapter, we'll take a look at some of the ways that practitioners of contemporary witchcraft move around in the world, crafting sacred spaces, using magical tools, creating magic with everyday objects, and recording their experiences through magical recordkeeping. Witchcraft attracts many kinds of people, but it is especially appealing to artists, creatives, and those with the ability to find power, beauty, and utility in overlooked or unappreciated places.

Altars and Sacred Space

For many reasons, we could assert that a core feature of contemporary witchcraft is an emphasis on embodiment. Witches often locate the sacred in the physical world, identifying as animists, pantheists, and as various kinds of polytheists that place gods and spirits in the physical environment. It is common for witches to treat plants, animals, the human body, stones and crystals, and natural bodies like rivers and mountains as innately sacred, powerful, or otherwise entitled to deep care and respect. The practices of witchcraft often center wellness, material prosperity, self-care, and building connections within an assortment of communities (including with the natural world). Both religious and non-religious forms of witchcraft prioritize the experiences of the human body (like sex, birth, and death) and our place within the wider material world. One of the most visible, pragmatic, and simple expressions of this rootedness in the material is the practice of building and maintaining altars.

Altars are physical spaces that have a few functions for the witches who maintain them. They contain objects that are important for the individual witch's practice, like working tools (more on those in the next section), various kinds of supplies and magical materials, symbols of devotion like statues or other kinds of artwork (if the witch works with a specific deity or spirit), and potentially myriad other objects that are personally or magically meaningful. Witches may change their altars to reflect the shift in the seasons, decorating them with gourds and pumpkins in the fall or fresh flowers in the spring. Some altars are dedicated to honoring the witch's ancestors and will contain items that represent each of those special people—perhaps their personal effects, photographs, and even food or drink they enjoyed while alive.

Many witches work within an elemental framework, ascribing cosmological significance to the four classical elements: earth, air, fire, and water. The altar—perhaps an unassuming shelf in a humble bedroom—becomes a miniature representation of the cosmos, with perhaps only four simple components: some soil or salt for earth, a dish of water, a lit candle representing fire, and a feather, censer, or other sort of incense burner to represent air. These simple objects represent their respective natural forces but also symbolize human attributes: in most systems, air is tied to the intellect and to knowledge, fire to the will and to passion, water to daring and to the depth of our emotions, and earth to silence, stillness, and rootedness. Not all witches work within an elemental framework, but for the many who do, this is a good example of how objects can take on both practical and highly symbolic dimensions. The items on an altar often hold multiple meanings and functions!

Some witches will choose soil, stones, or water from specific special places, such as a homeland, a sacred site (like a holy well dedicated to a particular saint, spirit, or deity), or an environment that otherwise reflects the witch's personal tradition. Many witches enjoy creating their own incenses or infused oils for scenting and anointing their sacred spaces, special tools, or their own bodies. These too are often stored on altars or in adjacent cabinets or on shelves. Candles are another near-ubiquitous feature on a witch's altar. In environments where witches can't use candles (perhaps in a dorm room or an apartment that doesn't allow fire), they may use artificial candles, string lights, or lanterns. These create a magical atmosphere but may also have additional significance for the witch. Just like in many religious traditions, candles are often lit to represent deities or spirits or to aid personal prayers or ritual workings.

For many new witches, their first act of witchcraft practice is the assemblage of a personal altar. This is a common piece of advice in how-to books, and a substantial proportion of online content entails the sharing of images and practical instruction with regard to the construction of altars and other kinds of sacred spaces. Both influencers and writers detail what objects to keep on an altar, where in the home to place an altar (especially if it needs to be hidden, perhaps because the witch lives in a shared space or has to keep their practice secret), how to personalize it, and how to best organize spells and rituals using it. Practically any kind of surface can be transformed into an altar: nightstands, tables, shelves on a bookcase, plant stands, desks, dresser tops, coffee tables, log rounds, flat stones, and infinitely more. Some witches with the means to do so will construct or commission bespoke altars, crafted with their own traditions and needs in mind and installed permanently in their homes or outdoor spaces.

It's common for witches to maintain more than one altar, if they have the space to do so. Within one witch's home, you might find an ancestral altar, separate altars for individual deities, altars designed for particular purposes (like prosperity, protection, or love), and others, limited only by the creativity of the witch. Some witches will use the term "working altar" to designate the altar where they perform magic or that otherwise is the central focus of their ritual work. A working altar may be permanent, or it may be erected temporarily only for the course of a specific ritual. Often, altars are literally at the center of witchcraft rituals, placed in the middle of a magic circle or temple space to hold the witch's tools and any offerings for deities or spirits. Particular traditions of witchcraft might have parameters in place for what should go on an altar, what direction it should face, and even what size and shape it should take. When a witch has to travel, especially for an extended period, it's not uncommon for them to set up some kind of portable altar or else to bring small, key items with them to set up an altar at their destination.

The altar is a physical representation of the witch's personal practice, reflecting their aesthetic sensibilities, personal convictions, inner cosmologies, and also practical needs. Individual witches may have very different needs and goals, and so a lot of variety exists. Some witches feel no need at all to maintain an altar or similar designated magical spot and instead treat their whole physical environment as a potential working space. For these witches, their craft may be so thoroughly imbued in their homes that keeping an altar would be redundant. Their kitchen counter, dining room table, or bathroom vanity may double as a magical surface, as the need arises. Their supplies and tools live alongside their mundane belongings—a reflection of the perspective that many witches of all kinds hold: that the boundary between the mundane and the magical is illusory. Anything potentially becomes magical in the hands of a witch! Why use a cauldron and a ritual dagger when a saucepan and a trusty kitchen knife can get the job done just as well?

The altar is one example of a particular kind of sacred space that many witches create for themselves. If a witch is fortunate enough to have the personal space to do so, they may set up a whole room in their home as a kind of designated ritual space. If they have a yard, they may construct an outdoor space appropriate for working magic, clearing and decorating it appropriately. Most witches, however, quickly learn to take advantage of whatever space and resources they have available to them, whether that means simply moving the living room couch when it's time to work a ritual, only erecting an altar when they immediately need it, and otherwise learning to take up less space as life with roommates and family members makes it important to be as flexible as possible. Some witches who work outdoors don't feel the need to designate separate sacred space at all, feeling that nature itself is sacred and doesn't require any additional designation as such. Other witches treat the indoors and the outdoors the same, bringing the same tools, supplies, and ritual structures wherever they go to work magic.

Working Tools

The tools of witchcraft are many and varied, the possibilities limited only by the witch. There are, however, a few that consistently appear on many kinds of altars, in many traditions, and among many kinds of witches. Some of that ubiquity is related to our earlier conversation about the prevalence and influence of Wicca. Many of Wicca's primary tools find their origins in earlier ceremonial magic traditions—especially the black-handled dagger called the athame, the cup, the wand, and the pentacle—and other traditions of witchcraft have at times either adopted these from the same places, drawing from these same earlier sources, or else have been inspired by Wicca after the fact. Other tools, like the forked walking staff called the stang, are more specific to traditional and folk witchcrafts. Every individual witch assembles their own working tools and may make choices that apply only to them and their unique practice. Some witches eschew formal working tools, instead relying on their own minds and imaginations, and using the everyday objects that are already present in their environments. Here are some of the tools that you are likely to encounter, along with a bit about their uses.

Blades

There are several blades in witchcraft. Probably the most common is the black-handled, double-edged knife called the athame. In Wicca, the athame represents the intellect, knowledge, and wisdom. As a ceremonial tool, this dagger is typically not sharpened and is rarely if ever used to cut anything material. Instead it is a tool for directing energy. Wiccan witches use it to cast the magic circle within which Wiccan ritual takes place. Other traditions of witchcraft may also incorporate the athame for similar purposes, but some witches with a more pragmatic bent prefer other sorts of knives, keeping them sharp and using them to craft other materials in their practices—cutting herbs or cords, inscribing symbols into candles, and so on. Many folk witches use simple kitchen knives, feeling no need to separate their ritual tools from their mundane tools. Some witches use a special knife with a curved blade called a boline, often reserved for harvesting plants. You may also encounter swords in witchcraft, especially in traditions inspired by earlier ceremonial magic traditions. In Wicca, the sword is usually used by coven leaders in group rituals, rather than by individuals working alone. Like the athame, it is used to direct energy. Some witches don't use blades at all, but for others, magical knives are the most important tools, representing their own personal power and possibly a connection to their traditions.

Cups

Cups or chalices are often included in ritual for the purpose of offering libations to deities and spirits, as well as consuming wine, juice, or water in ritual. In some traditions, the cup carries symbolic associations; because it is a curved container designed for nourishment, it often is used to represent certain goddesses, motherhood, and femininity. Some connect it to the element of water, which is typically associated with the emotions, mystery, and deep wisdom.

Cauldrons

Cauldrons are typically made from cast iron and come in many sizes. If a cauldron is large, a witch may use it for lighting fires, brewing magical concoctions, and other tasks that involve having a safe, heatproof container. Small cauldrons may be used to contain burning incense or for igniting small items like slips of paper or dried herbs in spells. The cauldron often carries the same associations as the cup, as it is also potentially a vessel for liquids. Cauldrons are also particularly tied to wisdom, as they play a key role in the story of Cerridwen, a popular Welsh goddess who is a favorite among many witches.

Pentacles

The pentacle is a flat disc usually made out of wax, copper, or wood. It is inscribed with assorted symbols, most commonly the five-pointed star called a pentagram. The pentacle has a number of magical uses, some of which are unique to specific traditions. Most simply it may serve as a magically charged working surface for other operations and is often a symbolic representation of the element of earth. Pentacles come in a variety of sizes, may also be used in various kinds of charms, and are even worn as magical jewelry.

Wands

In witchcraft, wands are typically made out of various kinds of wood, each with its own unique magical or cultural associations, meaningful to the individual witch. In other magical communities, like ceremonial traditions or New Age traditions, you may encounter wands made out of metal, crystal, glass, or other materials. Like the athame, the wand is a tool for directing energy, and some witches use wands instead of blades as a matter of personal preference. In traditions that use both an athame and a wand, the wand may have additional tasks. Wands are typically tied to the element of fire and associated with the will, with passion, and with power. As a phallic symbol, the wand may also be associated with masculinity and is sometimes used as a representation of assorted male gods.

The Stang

Robert Cochrane, whom we met in an earlier chapter, gets the credit for introducing the stang to contemporary witchcraft, though both witches and scholars have attempted to point to an earlier history. This is a forked staff that in many forms of traditional witchcraft represents the Witch Father (sometimes called the Horned God), a deity of witches, the underworld, and the wild. The stang, like other tools we've encountered, is used for directing energy and for performing invocations. The witch may also use the stang in trance work, riding it or holding it to travel in spirit realms. Sometimes the stang serves as a kind of altar, with the witch posting it in their ritual space and adorning it with the seasons or for the specific purposes of the working.

Herbs

A great many witches enjoy growing and foraging for plants and may keep gardens or potted plants in their homes. Those who identify as green witches make it a central part of their practice. Plants have magical associations, some rooted in historical magical systems, and others intuitively or magically ascertained by individual witches. Many witches believe that plants have a consciousness of their own and work as our allies, assisting us in both magical and mundane ways: feeding us, healing us, and empowering us. Many newcomers to witchcraft begin by learning about plants and may gradually build their own collections of living and dried specimens. They learn to blend their own incenses, infuse oils, and incorporate plants into spellcasting.

Crystals and Stones

If you've spent much time on social media on witchcraft hashtags, you've probably seen a lot of images of witches with crystals. Polished crystals mined from various regions throughout the world are a comparatively recent component of contemporary witchcraft practice, rising to popularity at the end of the twentieth century through the works of popular witch authors and also the influence of the New Age. In practice, though, crystals and stones have magical and practical uses similar to those of herbs. Many witches feel that they have properties that magnify magical power and even have the capacity to heal. Witches may carry stones and crystals with them to attract or repel particular energies (for example, carrying rose quartz to draw love or black tourmaline to ward off negativity). They may place them on altars or use them in rituals to augment the energy that they raise. A growing number of witches are concerned with the environmental damage and humanitarian injustices that mining crystals often entails, and so they prefer to find stones in their own regions.

Animals

Some witches incorporate animal remains into their magical practice, including skulls and bones, whiskers, feathers, pelts, snake shed, antlers, and teeth. Like plants and crystals, these components are often thought to carry their own magical energy, which is useful in spellcasting (for example, using shed snakeskin in a spell to bring about personal transformation or fox fur in a spell to evade a bad situation). Many witches who use animal parts do so as a representation of particular deities and may even work with the spirit of that individual animal. Some witches incorporate animal remains symbolically in their rituals, pointing to cultural or personal associations. Most witches who use animal parts as a component of their practice acquire them secondhand, find them outdoors, or purchase them from sources they've determined to be ethical. Some witches forage or hunt. Meanwhile, many witches completely eschew the use of animals entirely (vegetarianism and veganism are popular among witches), and this can be a controversial topic in magical spaces.

Keeping Magical Books

Books occupy a privileged position in witchcraft communities. It's difficult to make generalizations or sweeping statements about witches, but if I had to pick one it would be this: we love books! Because witchcraft collectively is decentralized, individualized, and largely unregulated, most witches are dependent on learning their traditions and exploring new avenues for personal development through the consumption of various kinds of texts. Today, that's likely to include social media content like videos, blogs, and info posts, but books are still an important medium for learning. This is especially true for witches who don't have access to in-person communities, direct mentorship, or other kinds of social sharing opportunities. Since the rise of witchcraft's popularity in the mid-twentieth century, books have been the key to the spread of ideas in magical spaces. Whereas in earlier decades witches were reliant on comparatively fewer titles, by the 1990s a witchcraft publishing boom was underway. Today, there are literally thousands of titles for witches and the witch-curious to choose from, with more and more coming out every year. A trip to most any large bookstore will offer readers a choice of broad introductory texts, as well as an increasing number of works on very niche magical topics. Mainstream publishers have leaned into the rising popularity of witchcraft, and specialty metaphysical and occult presses offer their own tomes via the internet or through specialty shops, often in collectible, highly sought-after formats.

On social media, much of the conversation in witch spaces revolves around favorite books, controversial books, newly released books, and the authors and publishing houses that produce them. New witches often begin their explorations by asking for recommended reading, and more experienced witches (and fellow newbies) respond with vehemence, especially over what books to avoid. Expertise is often assumed based on what witches have on their shelves, and additional authority may be conferred on anyone who takes it upon themselves to write books. A personal turning point for many newcomers to witchcraft is the moment that they stop merely reading and actually try something—a spell, a ritual, a craft, an invocation—and this is the subject of many an enthusiastic social media post!

Beyond the mere acquisition and consumption of books about witchcraft and magic is the practice of writing and maintaining a personal book—an intimate sort of journal that may contain spells and rituals written by the owner, as well as diary entries and personal accounts of their individual practice of the craft. There are a few names that witches might use for this sort of book, as well as many variations on how individual witches actually use them. The term "Book of Shadows" is probably the most common. The poetic phrase appears initially in the 1950s with the works of Gerald Gardner, who described the book as containing the rites and rituals of the secret witch cult he purported to have been initiated into. Becoming an initiate into witchcraft entailed receiving access to this book, which would then be hand-copied by the new initiate so that each witch had their own personal version. For Gardnerian Wiccan covens today, as well as many related traditions, this continues to be true. Gerald Gardner produced several versions of his own Book of Shadows, as did Doreen Valiente and other witches writing near the same time. These books are highly guarded texts that still circulate among initiates in these lineages (and many controversies in the past have resulted from various people claiming to have illicitly acquired them, and sometimes even allegedly publishing parts of them). You may hear such witches speak of "The Book of Shadows" as a title, referring to the specific text sacred to their tradition. These books are sacred in the sense that they are special and set apart, and often there are rules in place about how they can be handled, shared, and modified. However, they are not revealed texts and are not the equivalent of texts like the Bible or the Qur'an. What makes them special is how they have been passed down by generations of witches, not that they are the words of deities or prophets.

Most witches do not rely on a specific, traditional Book of Shadows, however. Instead, they write their own! Even witches who are part of covens and traditions that do have a shared text are likely to keep their own personal Book of Shadows. These individual, personal books can be made from the humblest of spiral-bound notebooks to the priciest and totally bespoke examples of expert bookbinding. Over the course of their lives, each witch is likely to keep multiple books, just adding on as they grow and age. The contents of a Book of Shadows vary, but some common elements include information about the witch themself, records of attempted spells and their results, copies of favorite rituals, passages from favorite magical books or inspirational literature, photos and scrapbooking elements that document magical life, lists of magical correspondences, recipes, prayers and invocations to specific deities or spirits, family trees, and records of coven meetings. Every witch's book is totally unique to them, reflecting their personality, their values, and their creativity. Some witches keep three-ring binders instead of books, printing off their materials, and sorting them into sections. Others prefer to keep digital versions of their magical records, and you may hear witches joke about their "Blog of Shadows" or "Hard Drive of Shadows."

There are many purposes for a Book of Shadows. For some, as we've discussed, this represents a history and reflection of a tradition, passed from coven to initiate in a continuous line. For others, the primary objective of the Book of Shadows is one of personal reflection and growth. Just like a diary or journal, the Book of Shadows becomes a repository of stories, lessons learned along the way, and a record of personal transformation. Many witches keep their books for posterity, with the intention of passing them on to children or other family members, building a family-based tradition of witchcraft over time. It's an extraordinary honor and a great act of trust to inherit a Book of Shadows, and for many witches these books are their most cherished and well-used possessions. If you peruse social media for information about witches and witchcraft, you will very surely find posts about how to write more consistently in a Book of Shadows, ideas for decorating pages, and plenty of sneak peeks into individual personal books for the purpose of sharing inspiration.

Aside from the Book of Shadows, there is another form of magical book called a grimoire. The word "grimoire" has historically been used to refer to magic books that especially pertain to the conjuration of spirits, the construction of charms and other magical objects, and practical instructions for dealing with nefarious magic users and other potentially troublesome entities. Today, witches may use the terms "grimoire" and "Book of Shadows" interchangeably. Both contain spells, rituals, and instructions for performing various sorts of magical acts, along with tables of correspondences and information about various spirits. For many, the difference between the two is the personal, individualized nature of the Book of Shadows, which may be more similar to a diary. The grimoire is more like a manual, or a repository of knowledge, rather than a personal reflective text. Many witches also eschew the term "Book of Shadows" because of its ties to Wicca and the special additional meanings that the term carries in Wiccan spaces. Witches with roots in other traditions, like ceremonial magic or other forms of European occultism, may use materials from specific historical grimoires in their practices. Many published, circulating grimoires contain information about working with demons, angels, and other sorts of culturally specific entities. Examples of popular grimoires include *The Key of Solomon*, *The Sixth and Seventh Books of Moses*, and *The Book of St. Cyprian*. Witches pull from all of these and more, and they also compose their own grimoires detailing their own systems of practice over time.

Magic in the Mundane

In this chapter, we've covered many of the customary tools and their typical uses, along with the construction of sacred spaces and magical recordkeeping. This is enough to be able to recognize some of the most fundamental material practices of most contemporary witches. However, the possibility for many more is always present! Witchcraft is a fluid, creative practice that fosters a lot of innovation, improvisation, and personalization. Individual witches come up with magical uses for all manner of mundane objects and tasks, imbuing potentially myriad seemingly unrelated aspects of life with meaning and power. Something doesn't need to *look* like witchcraft to outsiders in order for it to *be* witchcraft to the person using it or doing it. A witch who is also a musician might enchant their instrument, ritualize its care, and incorporate it into spellcasting. A dancer might do the same with their costumes and shoes or transform their performances into acts of magic, channeling the energy raised and directing it for specific purposes. A witch who loves to cook might center their magical practice around the kitchen, their ritual tools all doubling as cooking implements and the stovetop serving as the altar. In the hands of witches, potentially any endeavor becomes magical.

In the previous chapter, we discussed the role that belief plays in witchcraft and some of the various beliefs that witches hold. Witches differ on where exactly power lies in the various objects that they include in their practices. Some believe that plants and animals have their own spiritual or magical essences by virtue of being living things—beyond merely serving as symbols for humans—and those essences are retained after death. A sprig of rosemary, for example, aside from having all the mundane physical properties of scent, flavor, and texture, also possesses the *energy* of rosemary, which the witch can interact with, build a relationship with, and call upon using the plant in whole or in part. Similarly, substances like metals possess both mundane qualities—like conductivity, hardness, and color—and also specific energies that can be harnessed for magical purposes. Many witches are animists, believing that objects (in addition to living things) possess a kind of consciousness, innate energy, or magical power on their own, independent of the symbolic ties that we humans ascribe to them. For these witches, objects are never just objects, but allies, friends, and potential repositories of magical power.

Suggested Reading

From Scholars

Coming to the Edge of the Circle: A Wiccan Initiation Ritual by Nikki Bado-Fralick (Oxford: Oxford University Press, 2005)

This short work is an autoethnography of an American Wiccan coven performed by the group's high priestess, who happens to also be a religious studies scholar! Though its focus is not explicitly on materiality, the thorough examination of ritual practice is helpful for thinking about how tools, pageantry, and creativity function to facilitate religious experience for many types of witches (and Wiccan witches in particular).

Art of the Grimoire: An Illustrated History of Magic Books and Spells by Owen Davies (New Haven, CT: Yale University Press, 2023)

Owen Davies has a number of titles of interest to readers curious about magic, witchcraft, and the occult, and this one is particularly wonderful because of its extensive illustrations! Enjoy a survey of magical books throughout history and gain some additional context for how witches (and all kinds of other magic users) use them today.

The Thing About Religion: An Introduction to the Material Study of Religions by David Morgan (Chapel Hill: University of North Carolina Press, 2021)

David Morgan is a widely respected expert on the *thinginess* of religion, and this highly readable introduction is perfect for the curious, with or without a scholarly background. Morgan points to both magical communities (including contemporary witches) and mainstream traditions for examples of the many ways in which objects function in religious life.

From Witches

These titles represent some of the ways different kinds of witches build relationships with the material, either diving deep into specific tools or demonstrating how witches creatively bring magic into the everyday.

Blackthorn's Botanical Magic: The Green Witch's Guide to Essential Oils for Spellcraft, Ritual & Healing by Amy Blackthorn (Newburyport, MA: Weiser Books, 2018)

Thrifty Witchery: Magick for the Penny-Pinching Practitioner by Martha Kirby Capo and Vincent Higginbotham (Woodbury, MN: Llewellyn, 2023)

The Witch's Altar: The Craft, Lore & Magick of Sacred Space by Jason Mankey and Laura Tempest Zakroff (Woodbury, MN: Llewellyn, 2018)

The Witch's Book of Shadows: The Craft, Lore & Magick of the Witch's Grimoire by Jason Mankey (Woodbury, MN: Llewellyn, 2017)

The Magick of Food: Rituals, Offerings & Why We Eat Together by Gwion Raven (Woodbury, MN: Llewellyn, 2020)

Chapter 7

The Rules of Witchcraft

It might seem antithetical to consider that witchcraft has rules. In some ways, this is a controversial topic among witches themselves. The appeal of witchcraft for many is that it exists outside the mainstream, aspiring to transgress the imposed limits of the status quo and its often arbitrary expectations. For practitioners, the figure of the witch represents liberation, opposition, individual freedom, and boundless creativity. Surely no one becomes a witch because they want more restrictions in their life! Though this sentiment is true enough—and a great number of witches will loudly proclaim that they are unbeholden to anyone's authority but their own—contemporary witchcraft is not without its fair share of boundaries, taboos, and expectations for particular behaviors.

In the twentieth century, it was common for witches in the public eye to describe their tradition as "white magic" or "white witchcraft" to emphasize that their beliefs and practices were ethical, upstanding, and rooted in a desire to do good in the world. This was especially important for practitioners living in countries that had anti-witchcraft laws in place, as England did in the mid-twentieth century, and in cases where moral panic was directed at alleged occultists, as was the case in the United States during the 1980s and 1990s.[34] Most of the how-to guides from these periods assert that witches follow a strict code that prevents them from doing harm with magic.[35] Many witches who began practicing under the influence of these books continue to adhere to this narrative, actively eschewing harmful or manipulative spells. Today, however, the picture is somewhat more complicated (indeed, outside of the public eye, it is likely that the picture was always more complicated). Aside from the clearly problematic equation of goodness and morality with whiteness and of evil and immorality with blackness—racialized assumptions that contemporary witches are interrogating deeply and largely discarding—the rising prominence of disparate types of witches has revealed a wide swath of moral positions that any individual might occupy.

Some witches adhere to ethical systems that seem to echo those of more mainstream religions, focusing on doing good, being kind, and trying to master some of the baser impulses of being flawed human beings. Some avoid certain kinds of magic because they believe in innate metaphysical consequences (popular interpretations of karma circulate heavily in many mainstream spaces and are also popular among witches). Other

34. Gerald Gardner devotes an entire chapter of *The Meaning of Witchcraft* to a discussion of the Black Mass, in which he ardently refutes the assertion that witchcraft is tied to evil. See Gerald Gardner, *The Meaning of Witchcraft* (Newburyport, MA: Weiser, 2004), 169–94.

35. Consider Scott Cunningham's best-selling *The Truth About Witchcraft Today* (St. Paul, MN: Llewellyn, 1994), 37–42.

witches, however, see magic as essentially neutral, with its character and direction left up to the witch using it. People are not entirely good or bad, and neither is magic. Like electricity, it can be used beneficently or destructively. Some witches use the term "baneful magic" to describe those practices that are intended to cause harm directly (like curses and hexes) or are otherwise morally ambiguous, potentially manipulative, or physically dangerous (for example, because they involve handling toxic plants). Historically, the witch is as much tied to destructive magic and nefarious behavior as to healing and helping, and so a growing number of witches embrace both. That doesn't mean that they live without boundaries, though! In the following sections, we'll take a look at some of the rules—both formal and informal—that pervade contemporary witchcraft.

Redes, Principles, and Oaths

Some traditions of witchcraft do have widely agreed-upon codes that provide practitioners with ethical parameters for recognizing and defining correct behavior. Probably the most famous of these is what is called the Wiccan Rede. Understood very simply—as it usually is in both online spaces and in popularly published books about Wicca—the rede indicates that if an action does not cause harm, the witch may do as they will. It is phrased differently in different texts and articulated with a great deal of variation, but most adherents use it as a general guideline that encourages each witch to reflect on the consequences and motivations behind any given action, but especially magical action. Typically, it reads, "An' it harm none, do as ye will." You may also see the more direct "harm none." The history of the Wiccan Rede is somewhat contested, and it is by no means a universal tenet of Wicca, but it circulates widely both among Wiccan adherents and as the subject of critique from practitioners of some other kinds of witchcraft.[36]

Another example of a codified set of ethical parameters is the document "Principles of Wiccan Belief," which was composed in 1974 in Minneapolis by a group calling itself the Council of American Witches and widely circulated among both witches and contemporary Pagans of all kinds. The group was promptly disbanded, but the thirteen principles outlined therein continued to be influential throughout the remainder of the twentieth century. They include statements affirming the sacredness of nature, the existence of magic as well as its availability to all, a precise definition of what it means to be a witch (including the instruction to not cause harm), and also a denial of the existence of absolute evil.[37] "Principles of Wiccan Belief" is not so well-traveled among young witches after the first decade of the twenty-first century, but it is still an important set of guidelines for some Wiccan witches and does sometimes appear on websites and in books intended for beginner witches.

Other traditions of witchcraft—both Wiccan and non-Wiccan—may have other sorts of established, agreed-upon rules for members. Individual covens and solitary practitioners of all kinds are also likely to develop personal codes of conduct,

36. You can learn more about the Wiccan Rede and its complicated history by consulting Ethan Doyle White, "'An' It Harm None, Do What Ye Will': A Historical Analysis of the Wiccan Rede," *Magic, Ritual, and Witchcraft* 10, no. 2 (2015): 142–71.

37. Margot Adler, *Drawing Down the Moon: Witches, Druids, Goddess-Worshippers, and Other Pagans in America Today*, rev. ed. (New York: Penguin, 1986), 101–3.

whether rooted in their immediate experiences or developed in conjunction with cultural or magical systems that are important to those witches. One of the most pervasive rules is that of maintaining varying levels of secrecy, especially for witches who are in covens or are part of initiatory traditions. Some kinds of Wicca and traditional witchcraft require initiates to swear oaths to protect the spiritual mysteries and ritual practices of that specific tradition. The exact nature of those oaths is by itself normally private, and they may also contain statements about correct behavior, maintaining relationships with mentors or covenmates, honoring particular deities or spirits, and using magic for designated purposes. Such traditions and the witches who practice them are called "oathbound," and the consequences for breaking those oaths can be quite steep. Witches who are accused of being oathbreakers may be thrown out of their covens, excluded from social spaces, and publicly shamed and are often also believed to suffer spiritual or magical consequences.

Individualism and Personal Responsibility

However impossible it might be to pin down a singular, shared ethic among all the different types of witches working today, we probably come closest when we consider the collective, almost universal emphasis on autonomy, personal responsibility, and individual intrepidness. Core to practically any practice of witchcraft is the desire to assert one's individuality and grow one's personal power, whatever form that may take. For some, that means the acquisition of particular kinds of knowledge. It's very common to see witches on social media encouraging (and chastising) each other to "do your research!" Instead of relying on others to provide education and consuming books or online posts uncritically, contemporary witches pride themselves on a willingness to explore, experiment, dig into history, follow intuition, and come to their own conclusions. It's not uncommon for solitary practitioners to express either a disinterest or outright disdain for coven life or wider community participation as a whole on the grounds that working with others potentially amounts to being told what to do or otherwise being controlled. Meanwhile, witches in covens often don't recognize any sort of allegiance to a wider tradition, to other covens within the same tradition, or to the authority of anyone outside of their immediate network. Even within hierarchical groups that focus on teaching and training, individual members are autonomous adults who may come and go as they choose.[38] In short, witches rarely like being told what to do!

For many witches, practicing their craft is largely about coming into personal power. As in the self-help genre, many guides to witchcraft focus on developing self-esteem, embracing a direct connection to the divine or to the universe, trusting the innate wisdom of intuition over outside authority, and asserting the right to control one's own life. Online, witches are prone to speaking about their experiences in caveats like, "This is *my* way, but not *the* way," or "You have to find the right way for *you*!" The many kinds of witchcraft available consistently emphasize this sort of individualistic, personalized perspective. In cases where a witchcraft author, teacher, or internet content creator seems to be pushing a personal agenda too fervently, implying that one style or tradition is more valid than another or otherwise attempting

38. We'll discuss how covens work and the many types of groups that witches form in the next chapter.

to over-influence their followers, the response from the wider community is usually suspicion, direct callouts, and accusations of spiritual grifting.

Witchcraft becomes a route to individual agency, and this is one of the reasons why it tends to attract people who might experience disenfranchisement or marginalization in other parts of life. Part of that individual agency includes the magical ability to confront wrongdoing and injustice, especially when conventional aid is inaccessible, unsympathetic, or just inadequate. A witch might cast a spell to bring an abuser to justice, for example. They might use magic either to directly punish someone who has wronged them, or only defensively to deflect negative energy that has been directed at them by another.

Even where a tradition of witchcraft might teach that magic has consequences—either passive and impersonal repercussions or targeted punishments issued by deities or spirits for wrongdoing—the decision to use it still rests with each individual witch, with the understanding that they must take responsibility for whatever happens afterward. Some Wiccan witches, for example, believe the magical universe operates according to a system of threefold return, in which the energy of every action returns to the witch three times or magnified by three. Called the Law of Three or the Law of Threefold Return, this idea was especially popularized at the end of the twentieth century by prolific writers like Ray Buckland and Scott Cunningham. Despite its popularity, however, it has never been a universal Wiccan tenet, nor is it always interpreted consistently by people who adhere to it. For some, this admonition is quite literal, but for others it is a poetic way of reminding the practitioner that they must accept the consequences of their own decisions. Other traditions of witchcraft have no such guideline.

Community and Sincerity

Along with a shared emphasis on individual agency and personal responsibility, wider witchcraft communities are collectively concerned with the sincerity of the practitioners who take on a vocal role representing those communities, whether online or at in-person events, and at any scale. Time and time again in witchcraft spaces, we see anxiety surrounding the authenticity of self-proclaimed witches who enter the public eye. In some mainstream spaces, being a witch can lead to particular kinds of marginalization, and as we've seen, this leads to many witches choosing to keep their beliefs and practices private. In other spaces, however—like among witches themselves, in magical communities as a whole, and in some alternative communities—being a witch (especially a knowledgeable, powerful, or influential one) comes with a certain amount of social capital. This has become increasingly true as more and more of us live big chunks of our lives on social media. With the rise of influencer and hustle culture, more and more people are turning to the internet for side income or with the hopes of growing monetizable platforms and escaping traditional workplaces entirely. This sometimes leads to a certain level of suspicion around very public witches and also increases the sense of betrayal when a popular writer, blogger, or influencer quits witchcraft, especially as the result of religious conversion. These sorts of concerns lead to a lot of conversation around serving community, building up other witches with encouragement, and sharing freely with those practitioners (especially newcomers) who are understood to be particularly sincere.

At the individual level, witches often express the importance of demonstrating sincerity and commitment to a wider community by freely sharing information. The practice of "gatekeeping," which is a loose term that usually refers to the practice of withholding access to or information about magical practice, is a popular topic among witches. Many practitioners connect to others and demonstrate their willingness to contribute by openly sharing their experiences, making educational content, answering questions online, and otherwise making themselves available to others, even if they themselves are beginners. Refusing to gatekeep information—and calling out people who do, whether justified or not—is a way to signal belonging, as well as seriousness. Being accused of gatekeeping, clout-chasing, or grifting can result in a witch being ostracized or publicly ridiculed. None of this is unique to witchcraft communities, of course, but the prevalence of these kinds of concerns centering sincerity and community commitment point to informal, shared boundaries, as well as predictable consequences for their violation.

Witchcraft as Work

If you peruse witch books, blogs, and social media posts, one of the concepts that you're sure to encounter repeatedly is the notion that witchcraft is work. You might see more experienced practitioners admonishing newcomers to "do the work" or lamenting that there are so many who are only interested in witchcraft for the novelty and aren't willing to accept that "witchcraft is work." Similarly, beginner books often advise readers that witchcraft, for all its fun and excitement, is serious business and will require a lot of time and effort—almost always described in terms of work, labor, or sacrifice. Rarely is this consciously and deliberately framed as a community ethic, but even witches who assert that their witchcraft is unrestrictive, unregulated, and unbound by religious rules are very likely to emphasize the role that work must play in progressing magically and being perceived as serious by other witches. The pervasiveness of this attitude is such that it functions as a way of establishing both community and personal expectations for correct behavior.

So what do witches actually mean when they say that witchcraft is work? A few different things! Most simply, among witches this is a reminder that witchcraft is an action—a thing that one actively does. Depending on a witch's individual tradition or style, this could mean ritual actions like marking a seasonal cycle with a coven, maintaining spiritual relationships with gods or ancestral spirits through offerings, casting spells, or engaging in a regular meditation practice. It might equally be a statement about intellectual engagement. Often, reading books, memorizing magical correspondences, learning the mythologies and languages that might be relevant to a specific cultural practice, and studying the history of witchcraft are all framed as doing the work. More abstractly, "the work" is also a metaphysical concept that echoes ideas that we've encountered in related traditions like Theosophy and the New Age, in which one of the goals for adherents is spiritual ascension or transformation. Through a process of mystical refinement and the acquisition of wisdom, an individual seeks to shed negative personal patterns, the baggage of previous incarnations, or a dependence on the material world, all in an attempt to come closer to the divine. For witches who understand themselves to be religious, a desire to connect with spiritual forces like deities might be central to the work of witchcraft, and they may also align with the ideas we see in these other religious movements.

For more witches, however, this process of learning to "do the work" is often more practical than mystical, focusing on living a more grounded, balanced life and growing emotionally, intellectually, and magically, rather than necessarily connecting with some conception of divinity. Doing the work often includes self-reflective practices like journaling and some kinds of conventional therapy in order to improve one's life and one's relationships with others. It may also include addressing one's fears and biases, learning to accept the consequences of one's actions, breaking patterns of generational abuse, resolving trauma, and developing a sense of community engagement. For many witches, doing the work is a social process. It might include taking part in particular kinds of activism and standing up for a variety of social justice causes, but it could also mean contributing to witchcraft communities directly by teaching, mentoring, leading groups, or running events.

The work of witchcraft might include any of the above, though it's worth noting that witches in conversation (especially on social media) rarely specify exactly what they mean by the term. Work takes on a magical, almost secretive quality, in which we can't necessarily verbalize the specifics, but we know it when we see it! The assumption is that a witch who is properly dedicated and invested will be visible to other witches by their personal energy, their comportment, their maturity, their success, or their reputation among other witches. More importantly, a witch who others believe is not doing the appropriate amount of work potentially faces social consequences like ridicule, exclusion, or other kinds of judgment.

Individual traditions of witchcraft—especially some forms of Wicca—might have specified ethical codes, rules, and expectations surrounding oaths and proper behavior. Sometimes those parameters are transmitted through aphorisms like the Wiccan Rede or through particular passages from a tradition's Book of Shadows, and sometimes they come through oral lore and direct mentorship. Sometimes behavioral parameters are adopted more organically, as individual witches explore particular traditions through solitary practice and consume books and online content from other practitioners sharing about their own experiences and personal beliefs. Collectively, however, witchcraft has few if any universal codes of conduct. Instead, we can speak of the loosely shared values described above: individualism, sincerity, and work. These are not ethical codes per se, nor are they rules. It is more accurate to think of them as repeating themes that point to shared values, however loosely defined or indirectly articulated. And just like any other group of people, individual witches ultimately make their own choices, may demonstrate inconsistency in how they behave over time, and may change their minds given the strains of particular circumstances. In the same way that we can't know for sure the direction of a person's moral compass in every potential quandary based only on their political or religious affiliation, being a witch doesn't entail adhering to a particular rule set or holding specific ethical positions. It only suggests some likely patterns.

Suggested Reading

From Scholars

Very little scholarly work exists that explicitly and directly addresses how contemporary witches think about morality, define personal values, or establish community codes of conduct. We do, however, have some works that consider boundary construction among witches, and these are helpful for learning about how magical communities might collectively think about shared ethics.

The New Generation Witches: Teenage Witchcraft in Contemporary Culture, edited by Hannah E. Johnston and Peg Aloi (Aldershot, UK: Ashgate, 2007)

This edited volume contains several essays about young people engaged in witchcraft, including some that touch on how teens approach boundaries, seek inclusion, and conceive of correct practice. As young people are perhaps the largest demographic drawn to contemporary witchcraft, several of the perspectives presented here can be extrapolated to think about the wider movement.

Eros and Touch from a Pagan Perspective: Divided for Love's Sake by Christine Hoff Kraemer (New York: Routledge, 2014)

Writing primarily from a theological perspective, Kraemer discusses how contemporary Pagans and witches conceive of the body as sacred through an exploration of touch, sexuality, and healing modalities centering the physical. For Kraemer, the body is a primary site for establishing a system of Pagan (and by extension witch) ethics, and her analysis is useful for thinking about some of the unconventional and unspoken ways that contemporary magical practitioners conceive of morality, beyond explicitly codified rules.

From Witches

These books represent a variety of positions when it comes to rules, ethical codes, and individual morals. Most books don't address this topic directly, but if you explore widely, you'll quickly see the many different positions that witches today hold.

The Modern Craft: Powerful Voices on Witchcraft Ethics, edited by Claire Askew and Alice Tarbuck (London: Watkins, 2022)

Ethics and the Craft: The History, Evolution, and Practice of Wiccan Ethics by John J. Coughlin (New York: Waning Moon Publications, 2009)

Of Blood and Bones: Working with Shadow Magick & the Dark Moon by Kate Freuler (Woodbury, MN: Llewellyn, 2020)

The Rede of the Wiccae: Adriana Porter, Gwen Thompson, and the Birth of a Tradition of Witchcraft by Robert Mathiesen and Theitic (Providence, RI: Olympian Press, 2005)

Utterly Wicked: Hexes, Curses, and Other Unsavory Notions by Dorothy Morrison (Newburyport, MA: Weiser, 2020)

Chapter 8

Witch Communities

Witchcraft is an expansive, even unruly, conglomeration of a lot of very different flavors and traditions. As you've seen many times over, there is no single practice, perspective, or lexicon that perfectly defines it. Even Wicca, which we can more neatly identify and describe based on its shared history and recognizable ritual practices, includes a number of sometimes very different varieties that have shifted in alternate directions over the decades of Wicca's development. All this unruliness means that witches collectively don't have one single way of organizing themselves and building communities. There's no one source of power and authority—like a pope, a council of elders, or elected leaders—that passes down declarations about who can do what or who's in and who's out. When someone decides to start practicing witchcraft, they don't have to get anyone's permission or sign their names to any official roster. And there's no one standing by to throw them out if they break any rules. How liberating! On the flip side, there also isn't a sanctioned support system doling out reliable education, providing a social safety net for members in need, or declaring and maintaining community boundaries and regulating belonging. Witches also sometimes have difficulty availing themselves of some of the legal protections and services offered more generally to religious practitioners, even when witches identify as religious.

However, just because witchcraft is so open, decentralized, and nebulous doesn't mean that community structures—both supportive and regulating—don't exist. Human beings can hardly help congregating, even if it's just to share their excitement over something that's important to them. Witches have found many ways to organize themselves, to share knowledge, to offer support, to police their shared boundaries, and to interact with other groups and state institutions. They build messy and sometimes massive internet communities, but they also form tight-knit in-person groups with strict codes of conduct. They start festivals and hold weekend conferences. Sometimes they file legal paperwork to start non-profit organizations or even churches. In this chapter, we'll take a look at all the ways that witches organize themselves and exist in community, both in groups and as individuals—even solitary witches engage in community, however indirectly. We'll also consider how authority works in witchcraft spaces. If no one is in charge, where do expectations about behavior come from? How do individuals become influential, determining what texts, traditions, and jargon are authoritative or just trendy? And on a more basic level, how do witches make friends and pass their traditions to subsequent generations of practitioners?

Covens

When Wiccan witchcraft first appeared in England in the middle of the twentieth century, Gerald Gardner and subsequent Wiccan practitioners described the movement—supposedly passed through antiquity—as being composed of a secretive network of loosely organized regional groups, called covens. The notion that witches gather in groups of thirteen, consisting of twelve witches and one officer to lead them, was popularized by archaeologist and folklorist Margaret Murray, writing decades earlier.[39] Though much of her scholarship about European witchcraft has been thoroughly dismantled today, Murray's influence on the contemporary witchcraft movement has been substantial. She had a massive impact, not just on Gardner, but on occultism as a whole, on the popular scholarship of the day, and on the witchcraft types that today we call traditional witchcraft. Sometimes through text analysis, we can trace her theories initially through the work of Wiccan witches and then watch as they make their way into other witch communities, such that their origins are forgotten or obscured, passed off as secret family history or folklore.[40] Witches organizing into covens is one example of this phenomenon. You've probably heard that witches in groups are called covens, but that term doesn't enter into common usage

39. Margaret Murray, *The Witch-Cult in Western Europe* (Oxford: Oxford University Press, 1921), 190–97.

40. Today, Margaret Murray holds the paradoxical distinction of being almost universally dismissed and derided in popular discourse among witches, all while some of her ideas continue to circulate authoritatively and unattributed.

until after Margaret Murray.[41] Today, however, it's common practice for witches of all types and traditions to form covens.

In some kinds of witchcraft, covens are very particularly organized and abide by strict rules. One example of this is the emphasis on gender balance that existed in the early days of Wicca. In Gerald Gardner's early version of contemporary witchcraft the coven was idealized to include not just twelve witches and one leader, but six couples and a high priestess or "Maiden."[42] In the early years of Wicca, people seeking to become witches were encouraged to approach a coven and ask for membership with a partner of the opposite gender, usually a romantic partner. This was thought to accomplish several things. First, it was thought to mirror the polarity of nature and of the divine feminine and masculine embodied in the Wiccan goddess and god, creating symbolic balance and a stronger foundation for ritual magic. Second, because many of the rituals circulating included gendered roles for ritual participants, it more easily ensured their performance, both in the coven itself and between the couple working on their own. Finally, it ensured that each priestess who may leave the coven to start her own—in a rite of passage called hiving—would

41. The word itself is Scottish and appears for the first time in the confessions of accused witch Isobel Gowdie in 1662 and subsequently in texts pertaining exclusively to the appearance of witchcraft in Scotland. Its prevalence in England is contemporary and due in large part to Murray's work. Read more in Ronald Hutton's *The Triumph of the Moon* (Oxford: Oxford University Press, 2019), 104.

42. Gerald Gardner, *Witchcraft Today*, 50th anniv. ed. (New York: Citadel Press, 2004), 125. A more thorough description of the supposed organization of the witch cult is provided in the first chapter of Gardner's subsequent volume, *The Meaning of Witchcraft*, originally published in 1959. Margaret Murray even wrote the introduction to *Witchcraft Today*!

do so with a consort to serve as her high priest. The high priestess would lead the coven, assisted by her partner, training new initiates in the art of witchcraft until they either were prepared to hive or else remained in the original coven as experienced elders.

As you can imagine, this is a very restrictive way of doing things and posed a number of problems as witchcraft as a whole rose to popularity. First of all, most aspiring witches—both then and now, Wiccan and non-Wiccan—don't come in pairs (let alone cisgender, heterosexual, married pairs). Even covens that wanted to adhere to this structure had difficulty doing so; thus, change and variation sprang up almost immediately to accommodate single practitioners and those with partners who didn't want to follow them into witchcraft. Second, this is a really limited model of gender that just isn't reflective of how most witches actually perform magic, both then and today. Many traditions don't emphasize gender at all, and may even actively subvert it as a social construct. Even initiatory Wicca, which has a history full of gender-based coven structuring, has shifted and expanded to include other models. Today, there are several traditions of witchcraft that are explicitly open only to particular communities and groups of people, such as women or gay men. A growing number of witches today see witchcraft as inherently an expression of queerness, and their own coven structures are likely to reflect this.

Covens today take many shapes and have many purposes. Some are highly structured, hierarchical, and exclusive, focusing on the formalized magical or religious training of members. They may be very small groups consisting of a membership in the single digits and led by a single leader who is in charge of determining coven activities. This type of coven is often appealing for practitioners who learn best in well-scaffolded, ordered settings. It allows for direct teaching and individualized attention in a learning environment. It also encourages the formation of deep bonds, which facilitate more powerful magic and ritual. Such small, intimate groups may operate like families (indeed, they may even actually *be* families), and thus are prone to being private, difficult to join, and even outright secretive. Coven structure is heavily determined by the nature of the specific tradition and the goals of the people involved. Some entail lengthy screening periods for potential members and initiation rituals open only to adults, but others are family oriented and celebratory, including children and even visiting non-witches. Some covens are deeply invested in community support and emphasize strong social relationships among members and outreach with wider local communities. In addition to magic and ritual, members may perform community service or host events for the public.

Many covens are egalitarian and flexible. They might still be relatively small but perhaps are eclectic in nature and less focused on teaching a particular tradition. Some covens rotate leadership or operate democratically, with no single person being in charge. They may create new rites and rituals together, learning out of books and from each other. Covens are often born out of an individual witch's desire for community. They begin when one person meets another, they choose to practice together, and then they add new members over time. Covens may advertise for members online, through in-person networks, or even through local periodicals. Some covens are short-lived, and others survive for decades, changing membership (or not!) over the years.

The word "coven" has also broadened as time has passed and now is often used to refer to groups of witches that may not resemble the small groups that initially formed in the mid-twentieth century among Wiccans and traditional witches. Some covens are "open" (as opposed to "closed")—available to participants freely, with no requirement for commitment or extensive rules for belonging. They may advertise publicly and welcome all comers, holding rituals in public spaces like parks or renting rooms in community centers, Unitarian Universalist churches, yoga studios, or even bars and restaurants. More commonly, these types of groups are called open circles, and they may sometimes refer to themselves as groves, circles, outer courts (as opposed to inner courts, which are not open), or by terms unique to the witches forming them. But "coven" has a lot of popular appeal and is used more broadly with each generation of incoming witches. You may even encounter online communities—social media groups, fan communities centering a popular witch influencer, feminist or metaphysical book clubs, and more—that refer to themselves as covens.

Solitary Practitioners

Though the idea of witches operating in covens was a significant component of how people approached witchcraft throughout much of the twentieth century, plenty of precedent exists for the witch as a lone figure practicing their art either hidden away in the woods or secretly amidst the unsuspecting townsfolk. If you're like me, you grew up hearing more stories about solitary, evil witches tormenting princesses and children than about groups of witches operating in complex networks, so the idea of the solitary witch might feel the most familiar. We also have plenty of imagery throughout literature and art depicting witches as village wise people, doling out cures, assisting with pregnancy, or serving as matchmakers. Indeed, the overwhelming majority of witches today are not a part of any covens and practice their magic alone. This is the result of both practical circumstance and personal preference. Most aspiring witches begin their explorations independently, inspired by media or personal experiences, and may or may not ever find other practitioners or groups available to join. Witches who are somewhat isolated may have less opportunity for in-person community, and they may be unable or unwilling to travel to meet others. If a witch is a busy parent, has a demanding profession or home life, is chronically ill, or lives in a conservative or high-risk area, they may be unable to consider coven life. And a lot of witches simply prefer being solitary and wouldn't join a coven even given the opportunity!

Many witches today practice magical traditions inspired by British cunning craft, a general term for the folk healing and magical practices of medieval and early modern Britain. Other regions both within and without Europe had their own names for similar practices, and what records we have of these traditions have been instrumental in both preserving and developing the magical systems we now think of as witchcraft. Whether or not these earlier healers and practitioners of the magical arts would have thought of themselves as witches, they have served as models for many witches today.[43] Contemporary witches inspired by regional folk customs and beliefs (whether inherited or adopted) as we saw in chapter 3 might refer to themselves as folk witches

43. And definitively many of these earlier practitioners would not have thought of themselves as witches. Much of what we know indicates that cunning folk in Britain were largely focused on *combating* witches and saw them as a different class of magic-users. For more, consider Ronald Hutton, *The Triumph of the Moon* (Oxford: Oxford University Press, 2019), 87–115.

or folk practitioners but are also likely to call their practices traditional witchcraft.

In Wicca, which as we saw earlier in this chapter initially centered the coven model, the development of strictly solitary practice was something of a revolutionary concept. Writers like Doreen Valiente and Ray Buckland—both Gardnerian initiates—had previously advocated for self-initiation and the development of ritual liturgy for solitary Wiccan witchcraft, but with the publication of the wildly popular *Wicca: A Guide for the Solitary Practitioner* by Scott Cunningham in 1989, solitary Wicca quickly became the norm. Cunningham was an American Wiccan who had learned to practice a tradition of witchcraft related to Gardnerian Wicca while a young man in California but then went on to practice alone. The idea that one could practice Wicca—previously an exclusive tradition with secret components revealed only to initiates—on one's own, aided only by books and one's creativity and intuition was extremely controversial in some Wiccan communities. The validity and authenticity of solitary practice within Wicca was a matter of intense debate throughout the final years of the twentieth century.

Despite this controversy, once several explicit guidebooks to this type of practice were on the shelves of major bookstores (and as more materials circulated freely on the burgeoning internet), solitary Wicca's popularity exploded. Infinitely easier to learn about and practice, solitary Wicca dominated both popular conversation and the book market. Cunningham's enormously influential texts have since led hundreds of thousands of people to explore Wicca, as well as other kinds of witchcraft and occultism. He is a widely beloved figure, and his works are some of the most steadfast on suggested reading lists circulating among the witch-curious.[44] Now, we tend to take solitary and eclectic forms of Wicca for granted, perhaps even ignoring initiatory strains, but this represented a major change in the movement as a whole.

Solitary witchcraft of all stripes is appealing because it creates a great deal of freedom for the practitioner. With no one else standing by to demand consideration or offer critique, the solitary witch can make choices purely for themselves. With so many resources now available for all kinds of individual practice, the would-be solitary practitioner has a near infinite selection of pathways to choose from. They can experiment freely, create new rituals, blend traditions, and explore on their own time, unbeholden to other witches. Being solitary, however, doesn't mean that an individual witch is entirely without community. These sorts of witches are still likely to participate in online communities and to exchange ideas with other practitioners informally, and they may still rely on mentorship or other types of education directly from other witches. There are numerous correspondence courses in witchcraft that have been available over the decades, designed for solitary practice from a distance, and more and more of these have appeared as the popularity of witchcraft on social media has grown. Solitary witches may also periodically attend public rituals, festivals, and conferences. For most witches, the dichotomy between solitary and group practice is a spectrum rather than a hard binary. Witches in covens do not perform all their workings in a group context, and solitary witches are rarely

---

44. While Cunningham was formative for many witches, myself included, it is important to understand that his works no longer reflect current understandings of witchcraft development and practice from a historical perspective. Readers should approach his books with this in mind.

completely reclusive. Many witches will fall into both categories at different points in their lives.

Festivals and Conferences

While it's absolutely true that not all witches are Pagan, the overlap between contemporary Pagans and witches is substantial, and one of those overlaps exists in the role that festivals have played in the development of both of these movements, especially in the United States. With roots in the counterculture of the 1960s and also much earlier in the Spiritualist gatherings of the nineteenth century, Pagan festivals are opportunities for practitioners of myriad traditions (all loosely fitting under the various umbrellas of "Paganism" or "alternative religion" or "spirituality") to come together and share workshops, rituals, and time away from the stress of the mundane world. Witches of all types represent a substantial presence at Pagan festivals, and the ideas and techniques that circulate in these spaces often have broader impact, as they subsequently make their way into the books, blogs, and social media posts written by attendees after the fact.

Very often these events are held outdoors and entail camping or sharing rustic cabins at rented summer camps. Some festivals have been extant for decades, the number of attendees and the programming offered—which might consist of anything from hand-drumming to using divination tools to writing rituals to effectively communicating with deities—fluctuating as interest in magic, Paganism, witchcraft, and spirituality shifts. Practitioners travel extensive distances to spend as long as a week surrounded by community, learning from one other, sharing their own knowledge through presentations of their own design, and volunteering their time to carry out various administrative and manual tasks to keep the festival running for the lowest cost possible. Most of these events are annual and run as extensions of Pagan and magical non-profit organizations, with regular members attending year after year. Many festivals invite prominent authors, ritualists, and teachers to speak and lead rituals for attendees, and also provide space for artists and craftspeople to vend their wares. Practitioners who may not have access to quality magical tools and art have the opportunity to buy and barter directly for them.

As Pagan and witchcraft communities as a whole have grown, the nature of festivals has also shifted, both in content and in venue. Reminiscent of comic and fan conventions, more and more magical events have come inside in recent years, taking over hotels and convention centers near or in major cities and offering attendees more of the comforts of home as they attend lectures, workshops, and rituals. Where camping festivals tend to be longer affairs, most indoor conferences take place over the course of weekends. They similarly feature presentations by Pagan and witch authors, content creators, leaders, and ritualists. Attendees come to learn, to connect, to shop, and to relax in shared magical space. We have also seen the development and rise of virtual events. Online gatherings allow practitioners from all over the world to come together without leaving home at all. Aside from increasing the accessibility of magical conferences, online gatherings have also allowed for the development of more niche events, with less crossover into other spiritual communities. While it was common to congregate under broader banners and attend festivals with Pagans, New Age practitioners, and other adjacent communities, recent years have birthed online events that cater to specific types of witches or specific aspects of magical practice. For many witches, festivals and conferences are their first opportunity to interact with wider magical communities. They continue to be important venues for the transmission of ideas and for the growth of witchcraft as a whole.

Social Media and the Internet

The internet and the rise of social media have dramatically impacted how witches of all kinds build and participate in community. While many witches in the mid-twentieth century aspired to belong to covens, more and more preferred to remain solitary as the decades passed and that possibility became more readily achievable. Would-be witches no longer had to seek out experienced practitioners to learn and could simply go to their favorite bookshop or library to pick up a guidebook intended for solo use. With the advent of the internet, the witch-curious no longer even needed to leave home. The end of the twentieth century and the beginning of the twenty-first saw the explosion of websites, message boards, and email LISTSERVs circulating information about witchcraft and creating opportunities for witches to interact with each other virtually. The rise of blogging and video platforms further personalized the online experience, allowing all sorts of users of all ages and levels of experience to share parts of their magical and religious lives. Witches turned to the internet to learn, to share their own progress, to argue with one another, and to find new ways to practice.

Today there are witchcraft communities that are exclusive to the internet, and sometimes these have minimal overlap with in-person communities. Virtual covens stream rituals, individual social media posts may function as acts of magic, and developer-savvy witches build specialized programs to perform divination and create online temples. Over time, as so many more newcomers enter through the internet rather than through books or direct mentorship, the internet has developed its own jargon, its own body of popular techniques, and perspectives that are relatively confined to social media. Because the internet is dramatically more accessible than other kinds of community, the content that circulates online often has greater reach and more impact than the ideas prevalent at in-person festivals or among witches who have learned primarily from either books or traditional coven training. The witch influencer or popular content creator potentially has as much or more impact on other practitioners as a venerated elder, an author, or a community organizer had in previous decades. As our collective dependence on social media and the internet grows, and as more newcomers learn through these new means, it is possible that we will see more divergence between in-person and online witchcraft communities. Already, marked differences exist, sometimes causing generational dissonance between older and younger witches (for example, differences in vocabulary, the circulation of different texts, and an emphasis on different values and social causes). The internet has been an enormously beneficial force in contemporary witchcraft, but it has also created unique challenges.

Authority and Influence

With decentralization and personal authority seemingly witchcraft's most consistently discernible characteristics, you might expect that as a collective movement it would be difficult to regulate and influence. If no single power structure exists and there are no officially recognized leaders, then where do rules come from? How does change happen? How does witchcraft grow and develop? How is it that all of the varieties of witches have enough in common that we can recognize the continuity of something like tradition? Witchcraft as a whole may not have official leaders, but as a community, witches do have various kinds of authorities who exert influence, inspire trends, and directly or indirectly help to enforce norms and boundaries. As much as autonomy and individualism are valued, witchcraft communities are as subject to cultural transmission as any other group. In some ways, especially since witchcraft today is also a trending consumer market that has intersected with the mainstream, witches are even more subject to certain kinds of social influence than other groups.

In the immediately preceding section, we discussed how social media has altered witchcraft communities. Magical influencers use social media to sell everything from books, ritual tools, and magical services like tarot readings and mentorship sessions to soaps, teas, clothes, and travel experiences. Newcomers to witchcraft, especially teens and young adults, emulate their favorite witch content creators, as well as the fictional witches who star in both popular literature and film. Trends in both practice and aesthetics circulate quickly, not unlike trends in music or dress. A trending hashtag can impact how whole generations of witches (regardless of whether they are solitary practitioners or participate in groups) are setting up their altars, what deities witches are discussing most, and whether or not a particular magical technique is popularly deemed to be acceptable or not. Witchcraft communities don't necessarily need sanctioned authorities or official regulations to establish the boundaries of their communities, discourage deviance, and develop a shared language. Individual practitioners reinforce or discourage particular behaviors and modes of thinking through the ways that they engage with each other, especially online. Practitioners with especially large or engaged platforms tend to have more influence than those without, and it is common to see shifts in online witchcraft communities that correspond to the content shared by such practitioners.

Even before the internet, however, witchcraft communities have been subject to a comparable kind of self-regulation through the influence of other kinds of authorities. One of the most significant of these is authors. Even where intuition, nature, and personal experience are emphasized, witchcraft remains heavily reliant on the circulation of books and other forms of text. Witches tend to be readers—books are a popular talking point on witch social media and at festivals—and this means that some of the most popular and well-known figures in witchcraft spaces are writers. Favorite books can exert as much influence as popular content creators, and the information contained in them is often heavily circulated in other media: for example, transformed into memes, pirated on websites, turned into short-form video, or read aloud on streaming platforms. The most popular speakers at witch and Pagan festivals and conferences are authors, and authors who are also content creators are likely to command larger social media followings than those practitioners without books to sell. You may sometimes hear the expression "Big Name Pagan" (BNP) to describe these practitioners, who dominate metaphysical stores and the spirituality sections of major booksellers. An individual witch may never participate in covens or other types of groups, either in-person or online, but they are likely to still reflect the ideas and practices of other witches through the books that they consume.

Witch communities are diverse and vary according to tradition, region, generation, and purpose. Most witches participate in multiple kinds of community over the course of their lives, and the types of communities that witches create shift as witchcraft itself grows and changes. Some groups may look and function similarly to religious or cultural institutions that you recognize, especially as some witches strive to obtain legal protection through their state or federal governments. If you explore either online or at public events like festivals, you are sure to encounter solitary practitioners and witches who belong to covens, but you will also find witches who embrace the language of "church" or form charitable non-profits. In ongoing efforts to legitimize various witch and Pagan traditions, many have adopted Protestant models and language, a necessity in a political climate that assumes Christianity (and particularly Protestant Christianity) as normative. This has been especially true among Wiccan witches. Meanwhile, online communities abound, some tightly regulated and long-standing and others open and constantly rotating membership (and many without clear boundaries around what it means to be a member at all). Whatever the case, personal authority, individual exploration, and creative freedom remain central ideals.

Suggested Reading

From Scholars

Solitary Pagans: Contemporary Witches, Wiccans, and Others Who Practice Alone by Helen Berger (Columbia: University of South Carolina Press, 2019)

A systematic overview of solitary practitioners of both witchcraft and Paganism by a long-respected sociologist working in Pagan studies.

Cyberhenge: Modern Pagans on the Internet by Douglas Cowan (New York: Routledge, 2005)

A somewhat dated text, given the rapid expansion of the internet, but still really valuable for understanding the role that online communities and tools have played in the spread and development of both witchcraft and Paganism.

Earthly Bodies, Magical Selves: Contemporary Pagans and the Search for Community by Sarah Pike (Berkeley: University of California Press, 2001)

An engaging, incredibly useful ethnography of Pagan festivals. This book is not about witchcraft explicitly, but witches have been heavily involved in the Pagan festival movement for decades, and many of Pike's interlocutors are witches of various types.

From Witches

Each of these books provides valuable insight into how witches participate in and build community, in its various forms. Given Wicca's emphasis on the coven, note that books about covens tend to be written from Wiccan perspectives.

Book of Shadows: A Modern Woman's Journey into the Wisdom of Witchcraft and the Magic of the Goddess by Phyllis Curott (New York: Broadway Books, 1998)

The Small-Town Pagan's Survival Guide: How to Thrive in Any Community by Bronwen Forbes (Woodbury, MN: Llewellyn, 2011)

Covencraft: Witchcraft for Three or More by Amber K (St. Paul, MN: Llewellyn, 1998)

Raising Witches: Teaching the Wiccan Faith to Children by Ashleen O'Gaea (Franklin Lakes, NJ: New Page Books, 2002)

The Real Witches' Coven: The Definitive Guide to Forming Your Own Wiccan Group by Kate West (London: Element, 2003)

Chapter 9

Witches in Conversation

Over the course of this book, we've discussed what witches practice and believe. We've learned about how magic works and described some of the tools that are involved. We've examined the many kinds of witchcraft that exist and how witches organize themselves into different kinds of communities. We've also considered how witches define religion, spirituality, and practice. In this final chapter, we'll take a brief look at some of the pressing conversations that concern witches, often coming up over and over again in different forms with succeeding generations of practitioners. Like many communities—from religious groups to professional organizations—controversies sometimes bubble and individual members may come down on various sides, finding either solidarity or opposition as they participate in a wider magical world. In many cases, these concerns reflect wider trends in their immediate political and social landscapes.

Belonging and Authenticity

There seems to be something fundamentally rooted in the experience of being human that demands that we seek belonging. Even the most curmudgeonly of us requires community to survive. We've structured our societies in such a way that, indeed, practically none of us even has the choice. We need each other! And on top of basic survival, for the sake of our own individual emotional development and our pursuit of joy, we want friends, we want to be perceived as valuable, and we want to be included. This impulse commonly comes to the fore when we enter into new communities and seek respect and validation. We want to be treated as sincere, authentic, and real. This is true in communities based around hobbies and fandoms, and it's also true in religious and magical communities. Debates over who is and is not a real member of a group rage in practically any sphere we could imagine, especially when someone is accused of bad behavior or other sorts of controversy are afoot.

The conversation around who is and is not a real witch has been prominent in contemporary witchcraft spaces since these communities entered the public eye. Regardless of tradition or type, many witches experience strong emotions around where the boundary between insider and outsider lies. When Wicca came to the fore in the latter half of the twentieth century, the mark of belonging was a formal initiation ritual at the hands of another initiated witch to bring the new person into the craft. When writers like Doreen Valiente, Ray Buckland, Scott Cunningham, and Silver RavenWolf began publishing work about solitary practice and even self-initiation—which enabled potentially anyone to induct themselves as Wiccans—not everyone was enthused or supportive. Debates over whether or not someone needed to be initiated into a coven in order to be a witch impacted not just Wiccan communities, but some forms of traditional witchcraft as well. Many traditional witches taught that one needed to be adopted into a witch family or initiated into a specific magical system (sometimes called a current) in order to truly be a witch. With the boom in popular publishing and then the advent of the internet (and later social media), information was infinitely more available. This represented a major shift in witchcraft as a whole, and these debates haven't dissipated as the decades have passed.

The vast majority of practitioners today are not formally initiated into covens or specific lineages, but that doesn't mean that anxieties over authenticity have abated. Other measures are sometimes used, including whether or not a witch has read particular books (or, scandalously, prefers to consume online content rather than read books at all), whether they are willing to engage in particular magical practices that carry social currency in the moment (the idea that real witches shouldn't balk at the use of blood, animal remains, or bodily waste in spellcasting holds sway in some communities), or how frequently a witch engages in magical practice (both books and the internet abound with instructions for building as consistent and regulated a routine as possible in order to be the most effective practitioners they can be). We've seen repeatedly how much variation exists across the many forms of witchcraft, and this means that witches never run out of things to debate. The anxiety over belonging and respect seems to be so essentially human, and it only becomes more pronounced among people who already tend to be highly individualistic, outspoken, and confident in their own personal power. No matter what sort of witch someone is, there is always another witch close by to tell them they're doing it wrong.

Selling Witchcraft

Whatever else witchcraft is, it's also a thriving consumer market. One *New York Times* article from October 2023 observes that practitioners selling psychic readings and spellcasting services are part of an industry worth more than two billion dollars, and that's excluding the revenue generated through content creation, book publishing, and the sponsored advertising produced by influencers.[45] Searching witchcraft hashtags on any social media platform reveals all manner of products aside from magical services, including clothing, day planners, visual art, jewelry, perfume, makeup, and home décor. Large general retailers stock how-to guides and even magical tools like incense, crystals, tarot cards, and pendulums. Beyond engaging in consumption, a growing number of witches express a desire to make witchcraft their profession, opening shops, manufacturing products in their homes, setting up tarot businesses, and offering mentorship to new witches in exchange for fees that range the entirety of the financial spectrum.

The relationship between witchcraft and money is complicated, both historically and among witches today. As we've seen, for a growing number of witches, their traditions are a craft, a skill set, and a trade. The religious, nature-loving devotee invested in personal transformation that we have seen come to the fore beginning in the mid-twentieth century sometimes bears little

45. T. M. Brown, "Practical Magic: The Lucrative Business of Being a Witch on Etsy and TikTok," *New York Times,* October 28, 2023, https://www.nytimes.com/2023/10/28/style/witch-tiktok-etsy-business.html.

resemblance to earlier figures described in witchcraft histories. The image of the village witch doling out spells and potions in exchange for payment from the local townsfolk has been with us for considerably longer, and this is the tradition that many uphold. In contrast, some forms of witchcraft (especially some forms of Wiccan witchcraft) teach that witches should never request payment for performing magic, as the witch is duty-bound to serve their community regardless of who can afford their skills. Some practitioners tread this boundary with nuance, charging for services like readings and spells, but not for magical training or healing. As with all things, individual witches set their own parameters for what they deem appropriate.

Beyond any personal moral convictions about money, there also arises wider questions concerning trust and exploitation. In an environment that already includes some anxiety around belonging and authenticity, introducing the incentive of potentially making quite a lot of money further complicates matters. It's common to hear witches speculating about who is sincere and who is just trying to capitalize on the fact that witchcraft is trendy. "They're just in it for the aesthetic" is an increasingly common insult. Social media abounds with critique not just of witch influencers and content creators, but also of witch authors and teachers, who are sometimes accused of taking financial advantage of their communities. Suspicion around practitioners who have found ways to make money being witches has existed throughout the twentieth century, even from practitioners who assert that witchcraft is a skill that warrants payment. The conversation surrounding what it means to sell witchcraft—and who may do it and how and for how much—is an old one but one that intensifies every time witchcraft comes back in style.

Social Justice

Like in the wider world, the concern for the unequal distribution of power, protection, and opportunity is rising within witchcraft spaces. Contemporary witchcraft is as subject to the effects of racism, sexism, classism, homophobia, transphobia, xenophobia, and other forms of oppression as any other community or social space, and these ills manifest in myriad ways. Some are overt, and they mirror patterns that we see in the overculture, like the dominance of white voices over those belonging to people of the global majority or the tendency to locate authority with men (even in spaces where women are the majority). A perusal of the available witchcraft-related books at a typical bookshop or the speaker roster at a typical Pagan conference or festival can reveal striking disparities in race, gender, and class. Other problems are more internal to witchcraft communities: for example, the emphasis on heteronormativity and traditional gender roles in many kinds of covens or the appropriation of Indigenous, Black, and Asian magical practices by the beneficiaries of white colonialism.

Thanks to the activist efforts of a number of highly vocal witchcraft authors and teachers, the practice of witchcraft for many is closely tied to political engagement. "Witchcraft is political" has become a slogan that circulates readily on social media, at witchcraft events, and in witchcraft books. Indeed, political activism may be a cornerstone of an individual witch's practice, and there are even some traditions (most notably Reclaiming) that centralize activism as not just necessary, but sacred. If witchcraft is a practice that belongs to the marginalized, then surely its best use is in defense of the marginalized. Witches discuss mass spellcasting on social media, working together to magically hex politicians or protect protesters. Networks of covens work together to dismantle gender essentialist concepts and trans exclusive language in long-standing liturgies. Magical publishers and online blogging and news platforms seek out and elevate marginalized voices, gradually shifting the narratives that we collectively tell. Witchcraft conferences and festivals introduce virtual programming to make their events more affordable and invest funds toward hiring a more diverse group of speakers and teachers.

All these efforts are slowly impacting contemporary witchcraft as a whole, making it more inclusive and equitable. Witches come from many sociocultural backgrounds, many geographic regions, and every age group, and their political beliefs, social values, and individual anxieties tend to reflect these differences. Conversations around social justice, activism, and political engagement are increasingly at the fore of popular conversations happening in witchcraft spaces, but that doesn't mean that witches clearly agree with one another on every issue. There is no singular witch perspective, any more than there is a singular kind of witch.

Many of the debates, controversies, and anxieties that arise in witchcraft spaces are not unique to these communities. Witches tend to be socially conscious, engaged people who feel strongly about their opinions, whatever those opinions might be. The emphasis on personal responsibility that characterizes witchcraft means that participating in wider community conversations is sometimes framed as a moral obligation, especially when individual witches feel that their personal efforts are for the sake of a greater good. The problems that impact wider society are no less present in magical communities, and individual practitioners address them in many ways. As witches, we are as guilty of and subject to the same social ills that impact other realms of life. Though many contemporary witches think of their traditions as innately progressive and believe that witches are wiser, more conscientious, and more self-aware than other sorts of people, the reality is that our communities collectively are as flawed as any other. In fact, the assumption that fellow witches must surely agree on matters of politics or social justice means that sometimes it takes us longer to root out bad actors in our communities, and we can be slow to address systemic injustices in our midst. The good news, however, is that witches by and large are committed to building healthy shared spaces, contributing to positive change in a wider world, and protecting and supporting each other. Every generation produces new ideas, new texts, and new resources to do just that.

Suggested Reading

From Scholars

Stealing My Religion: Not Just Any Cultural Appropriation by Liz Bucar (Cambridge, MA: Harvard University Press, 2022)

Through a series of case studies, ethicist and religion scholar Liz Bucar explores the impact of cultural appropriation in three different religious communities. This text will help readers better understand the subject as it unfolds in many other spaces, including among witches.

Gods of the Blood: The Pagan Revival and White Separatism by Mattias Gardell (Durham, NC: Duke University Press, 2003)

Though many Pagan and witch spaces are (or strive to be) anti-racist, politically progressive, and invested in many kinds of social justice, this is certainly not the case for all. Gardell introduces us to another current entirely, which has continued to grow since the publication of his research. Though it doesn't focus explicitly on witches, the histories and ideas presented in this text are relevant to all kinds of Pagan and magical practices, especially in the United States.

Indigenizing Movements in Europe, edited by Graham Harvey (Sheffield, UK: Equinox, 2020)

Here is a collection of articles concerning contemporary Paganism in both Europe and North America, indigeneity, and the politics surrounding notions of belonging. This text is useful for thinking about colonialism, land ownership, and the efforts that many Pagans, witches, and occultists make to establish continuity with the past.

From Witches

These books all directly address the many social problems that arise in witchcraft communities, providing perspectives from marginalized members as well as guidance for witches invested in social justice, environmental activism, inclusivity, and other forms of political engagement.

All Acts of Love and Pleasure: Inclusive Wicca by Yvonne Aburrow (London: Avalonia, 2014)

Earth Works: Ceremonies in Tower Time by H. Byron Ballard (Smith Bridge Press, 2018)

Bringing Race to the Table: Exploring Racism in the Pagan Community, edited by Crystal Blanton, Taylor Ellwood, and Brandy Williams (Stafford, UK: Megalithica Books, 2015)

Magic for the Resistance: Rituals and Spells for Change by Michael M. Hughes (Woodbury, MN: Llewellyn, 2018)

Revolutionary Witchcraft: A Guide to Magical Activism by Sarah Lyons (Philadelphia, PA: Running Press, 2019)

Witchcraft Activism: A Toolkit for Magical Resistance by David Salisbury (Newburyport, MA: Weiser, 2019)

Sacred Gender: Create Trans and Nonbinary Spiritual Connections by Ariana Serpentine (Woodbury, MN: Llewellyn, 2022)

Queering Your Craft: Witchcraft from the Margins by Cassandra Snow (Newburyport, MA: Weiser, 2020)

Becoming Dangerous: Witchy Femmes, Queer Conjurers, and Magical Rebels, edited by Katie West and Jasmine Elliott (Newburyport, MA: Weiser, 2018)

The New Aradia: A Witch's Handbook to Magical Resistance, edited by Laura Tempest Zakroff (Seattle, WA: Revelore Press, 2018)

Conclusion

I am more fortunate than many witches because I have always lived in areas with vibrant magical communities and have mostly been surrounded by people who were supportive rather than condemning and curious rather than dismissive. My parents certainly never intended for me to be a witch, and I'm sure they would have made other choices had I consulted them. I would wager, though, if you were to interrogate many of the people involved in my upbringing and early education, most wouldn't be terribly surprised when it came right down to it that I ended up here (or somewhere like it). Creative, willful, curious about the world, and excited by the prospect of other layers behind visible reality, at times I feel like my childhood self could have ended up nowhere else. Though it sounds cliché to my ears after living in these spaces for decades, it is also one of witchcraft's most cherished and oft-repeated narratives: discovering witchcraft felt like *coming home.* Once I knew that this was an option—a way to move through the world—I knew this was how I wanted to live.

My traditions have shifted over the years. I've been in covens, I've been solitary, I've used different terms to describe myself, and I've been more or less open about my identity as a witch in different stages of my life, but my craft has remained core to who I am. In witchcraft, I've found the room and the tools to create my own sense of meaning and purpose in a world that often feels disordered and violent. I've been encouraged to learn about the earth, building connections to the land I live on in ways that many people do not. I've also found my dearest and most long-standing relationships. Some are the close friends I've met at open circles, at festivals, and through the growing magical corners of the internet. Others are of the spiritual variety: my own ancestors and the ancestors of my traditions, the gods, the dead, and the spirits of the plant and animal kingdoms I live among. Through witchcraft, I've found the strength to navigate a variety of personal struggles, not because witchcraft is a cure-all, but because it's given me resources, connections, and perspectives that have encouraged me to act with compassion, to be honest with myself and others, and to take responsibility over those things within my control. In short, witchcraft makes me happy. It makes me *better*. And there are an awful lot of people who would say the same for themselves.

There is always more to say. There were many points during the writing of this book where I wished that I could neatly package a set of straightforward answers for you instead of so many winding and complex explorations that often amounted to the equivalent of "Well, it depends!" Is witchcraft a religion? Well, it depends! How do witches practice magic? Well, it depends! Ad nauseam, until you start to wonder if maybe it's not even possible to really know anything definitively at all. One of the great faults of so much of how we describe and understand the world today is the seemingly constant impulse to sort everything we encounter into neat boxes, building taxonomies and categorizing our surroundings—and the people in our lives—in such a way that we feel we've mastered them and can decisively say what they *really* are. In reality, all human beings are multidimensional, complicated, at times contradictory entanglements of ideas and experiences. We almost never check singular boxes and fit neatly into any stereotype.

Witchcraft defies direct, easy categories and concise answers. Perhaps that is why witches remain such mysterious, sometimes scary figures in the popular imagination: they instinctively transgress imposed boundaries. My goal here was never to nail witchcraft down, like an insect pinned under glass, but rather to provide you with a map that would allow you to more effectively encounter it in its own habitat, on its own terms. You will still find yourself sometimes stumped. You'll encounter individual witches who use different jargon and operate under different rules. You'll see religious combinations that seem implausible or impossible ("Why would someone *mix* those?"). You'll scroll through social media and see posts about the same tradition that disagree wildly, though each will be stated with the utmost authority and sincerity. You'll be sure you've got it figured out, and in only a handful of years the landscape will have shifted, such that you feel unmoored all over again. That is the nature of witchcraft. But now you have enough of the pieces to understand more of what you encounter, place it in context, and, most importantly, ask better questions.

If you read this book for the sake of loved ones who are practitioners, I hope knowing more about their beliefs and traditions strengthens your relationships. The efforts you make to understand people different from yourself go a long way to build a kinder, more just world. I hope that your now-shared vocabulary leads to more direct and honest connections and more empathy between you. As vocal and proud as many witches are today—building giant social media platforms, publishing books or blogs, leading open circles, and proclaiming their witchiness at their jobs and schools—many, many more exist in secrecy. Some continue to feel unsafe in their daily lives, hiding their craft from neighbors, coworkers, and even friends and family. Most of us live somewhere in between.

My own life as a witch has at times felt like living with a split identity, always negotiating which side I wear in any given moment. I have my legal, professional name, as well as my craft name—no mere pen name, but the name I chose as an excited newcomer desperately looking to step outside the mundane, which would solidify into a magical persona that sometimes seems to have a life of its own. Using one sometimes means obscuring or subverting the other. I make the choice based on how I wish to be perceived. As a scholar and as a professional, there are still powerful stigmas attached to being a witch. More than once someone in my academic network has found out that I'm a witch and said something like, "But you're smart! How could you be one of *those* people?" Decades ago, the concern may have been from various kinds of Fundamentalist Christian groups, but today I get the most flak from secular-minded folks who just think what I'm up to is sort of kooky. Isn't it just gullible, uneducated people who are into *that stuff*? To them I say that it's imperative we interrogate those things that we assume are normal, and that tell us that our way of moving about through the world is the most sensible and obvious. It's a big world, and we would see a lot more of it if we checked the impulse to dismiss people who find value in things outside of our own wheelhouse. I am vocal about who I am precisely because I know many more cannot be. The privileges provided through other parts of my identity—my whiteness, my education, my class status, my occupation—offer me protections that many other witches do not receive. If you think you only know one witch or that you don't know any, you're wrong. However vocal we may or may not be, I assure you we're working and studying and playing and voting and living alongside you.

The other half of that split identity manifests in those times when I use my craft name and walk in witch spaces, setting down the constantly critical perspectives fostered through my scholarly training. Scholarship is not inherently contradictory to practicing witchcraft (and scholarship is historically, collectively much less critical than it often imagines itself). I'm a scholar for many of the same reasons I'm a witch—I'm curious about the world and like having the tools to find my own answers. But scholarship is also often extractive, especially the ethnographic techniques that so many have relied upon in the past. It's also easy to misrepresent and to obscure witch communities with sociological data, especially when most scholars rely on questions better suited to normative religious traditions like Christianity and can only conduct their studies among visible, vocal practitioners. Witchcraft communities are large and diverse enough that if you look hard for a preconceived perspective or a foregone conclusion, you can find it. After a lengthy track record of mishandling by journalists and scholars, witches tend to be disinclined to open their doors to outsiders with an agenda (and those who are quick to talk are often subject to a fair bit of criticism from their peers). I have been a witch much longer than I have been a scholar, but I still find myself sometimes mitigating my presence in some communities with, "Don't worry, I'm not here to study you! I'm working on other things entirely." And while I wish that these types of reassurances weren't necessary, I certainly don't blame my communities for being at times suspicious. I maintain boundaries of my own whenever October rolls around and the interview requests arrive. I'll happily tell an academic narrative but leave the personal out. I'll discuss trends but not individuals. And when in doubt, I'll simply say nothing. Every time, the resulting newspaper or blog article will go in one of two directions: public reassurance of our normalcy or sensationalist clickbait. As always, the full picture can never be included in such short formats. Even a whole book can only ever be an approximation.

I hope that you've enjoyed this orientation to witchcraft and Wicca, and the intriguing, diverse people who compose these magical communities. The popularity of witchcraft, Wicca, magic, and the occult in public spaces waxes and wanes from decade to decade, but our numbers seem to be climbing with each generation. This means that more and more of the people you encounter in your own daily life may very well be practitioners, dabblers, clients, or just curious enthusiasts! You now have the tools to make sense of the trends, to understand the beliefs, to put magical practices in context, and to have informed conversations with people in these spaces. Witchcraft will continue to grow and change, attracting new voices, shifting vocabularies and community boundaries, articulating itself, and then breaking and growing into something new with each generation that practices it.

Bibliography

Adler, Margot. *Drawing Down the Moon: Witches, Druids, Goddess-Worshippers, and Other Pagans in America Today.* Rev. ed. New York: Penguin, 1986.

Coyle, T. Thorn. *Evolutionary Witchcraft*. New York: Penguin, 2004.

Cunningham, Scott. *The Truth about Witchcraft Today*. St. Paul, MN: Llewellyn Publications, 1994.

Durkheim, Émile. *The Elementary Forms of Religious Life*. Translated by Karen E. Fields. New York: The Free Press, 1995.

Freud, Sigmund. *Totem and Taboo: Some Points of Agreement between the Mental Lives of Savages and Neurotics*. Translated by James Strachey. New York: Norton, 1989.

Gardner, Gerald. *The Meaning of Witchcraft*. Boston: Weiser, 2004.

———. *Witchcraft Today*. 50th anniv. ed. New York: Citadel Press, 2004.

Heselton, Philip. *Doreen Valiente: Witch*. The Doreen Valiente Foundation in association with the Centre for Pagan Studies, 2016.

Hutton, Ronald. *The Triumph of the Moon*. 2nd ed. New York: Oxford University Press, 2019.

McGarry, Molly. *Ghosts of Futures Past: Spiritualism and the Cultural Politics of Nineteenth-Century America*. Berkeley: University of California Press, 2008.

Murray, Margaret. *The Witch-Cult in Western Europe*. Oxford: Oxford University Press, 1921.

Owen, Alex. *The Place of Enchantment: British Occultism and the Culture of the Modern*. Chicago: University of Chicago Press, 2004.

Pike, Sarah. *New Age and Neopagan Religions in America*. New York: Columbia University Press, 2004.

Satter, Beryl. *Each Mind a Kingdom: American Women, Sexual Purity, and the New Thought Movement, 1875–1920*. Berkeley: University of California Press, 1999.

Sulak, John C. *The Wizard and the Witch: Seven Decades of Counterculture, Magick & Paganism*. Woodbury, MN: Llewellyn Publications, 2014.

Three Initiates. *The Kybalion: Centenary Edition*. New York: TarcherPerigee, 2018.

Valiente, Doreen. *Witchcraft for Tomorrow*. London: Robert Hale, 2012.

White, Ethan Doyle. "'An' it Harm None, Do What Ye Will': A Historical Analysis of the Wiccan Rede." *Magic, Ritual, and Witchcraft* 10, no. 2 (2015): 142–71.

———. "Robert Cochrane and the Gardnerian Craft." *The Pomegranate: The International Journal of Pagan Studies* 13, no. 2 (2011): 205–24.

Index

About the Author

Thorn Mooney is a Wiccan writer and academic living in Raleigh, North Carolina. She holds master's degrees in both religious studies and English literature and is completing her PhD in religion and culture at the University of North Carolina at Chapel Hill. She writes and lectures about magic, new religious movements, and American religions for a wide variety of audiences. Thorn's professional background as a classroom teacher and as a scholar allows her to represent contemporary witch, Pagan, and occult communities from a critical perspective.

JAICO PUBLISHING HOUSE

Elevate Your Life. Transform Your World.

ESTABLISHED IN 1946, Jaico Publishing House is home to world-transforming authors such as Robin Sharma, Sadhguru, Osho, the Dalai Lama, Deepak Chopra, Eknath Easwaran, Paramhansa Yogananda, Devdutt Pattanaik, Radhakrishnan Pillai, Morgan Housel, Napoleon Hill, John Maxwell, Brian Tracy, and Stephen Hawking.

Our late founder Mr. Jaman Shah first established Jaico as a book distribution company. Sensing that independence was around the corner, he aptly named his company Jaico ('Jai' means victory in Hindi). In order to service the significant demand for affordable books in a developing nation, Mr. Shah initiated Jaico's own publications. Jaico was India's first publisher of paperback books in the English language.

While self-help; religion and philosophy; mind, body and spirit; and business titles form the cornerstone of our non-fiction list, we publish an exciting range of current affairs, history, biography, art and architecture, travel, and popular science books as well. Our renewed focus on popular fiction is evident in our new titles by a host of fresh young talent from India and abroad.

Jaico's translations division publishes select bestselling titles in over 10 regional languages including Gujarati, Hindi, Kannada, Malayalam, Marathi, Tamil, and Telugu. These include titles from renowned national and international authors like Sudha Murthy, Gaur Gopal Das, Swami Mukundananda, Jay Shetty, Simon Sinek, Ankur Warikoo and Jeff Keller.

Visit our Website

Boasting one of India's largest book distribution networks, Jaico has its headquarters in Mumbai, with branches in Ahmedabad, Bangalore, Chennai, Delhi, Hyderabad, and Kolkata. This network ensures that our books reach all parts of the country, both urban and rural.